A SHORT HISTORY OF
THE WOLF IN BRITAIN

BY

JAMES EDMUND HARTING,
F.L.S., F.Z.S.

To
Mr and Mrs. Dyson

From
Simran. K
2009

PRYOR PUBLICATIONS
WHITSTABLE AND WALSALL

PRYOR PUBLICATIONS
WHITSTABLE AND WALSALL

75 Dargate Road, Yorkletts,
Whitstable, Kent CT5 3AE
Tel. & Fax: (0227) 274655

Specialist in Facsimile Reproductions

MEMBER OF
INDEPENDENT PUBLISHERS GUILD

A full list of our publications
sent free on request

The publishers wish to thank
TITLES
old & rare books
15/1 Turl Street, Oxford OX1 3DQ
Telephone: (0865) 727928
for their co-operation in
this publication

ISBN 0 946014 27 2
©1994 Pryor Publications

Originally published 1880

A CIP Record for this book is available from the British Library

Printed and bound by
Whitstable Litho Printers Ltd., Whitstable

This book is dedicated to Lesley
in celebration of her life long
interest in the wolf

PUBLISHER'S NOTE

"A Short History Of The Wolf In Britain" is taken from James Harting's *"British Animals Extinct Within Historic Times"* published in 1880.

His book also covers The Bear, Beaver, Reindeer, Wild Boar and Wild White Cattle.

If there is sufficient interest forthcoming from the public the publishers will consider publishing the remainder of the book in this format.

THE WOLF.

Canis lupus.

OF the five species which come within the scope of the present work, the Wolf was the last to disappear. On this account, partly, the materials for its history as a British animal are more complete than is the case with any of the others.

To judge by the osteological remains which the researches of geologists have brought to light, there was perhaps scarcely a county in England or Wales in which, at one time or another, Wolves did not abound, while in Scotland and Ireland they must have been even still more numerous.

The vast tracts of unreclaimed forest land which formerly existed in these realms, the magnificent remnants of which in many parts still strike the beholder with awe and admiration, afforded for centuries an impenetrable retreat for these animals, from which it was well-nigh impossible to drive them. It was not, indeed, until all legitimate modes of hunting and trapping had proved in vain, until large prices set upon the heads of old and young had alike failed to compass their entire destruction, that by cutting down or burning whole tracts of the forests which harboured them, they were at length effectually extirpated.

In the course of the following remarks it is proposed to deal, first, with the geological evidence of the former existence and distribution of Wolves in the British Islands; secondly, with the historical evidence of their survival and gradual extinction.

Under the latter head it will be convenient to arrange the evidence separately for England and Wales, Scotland, and Ireland: and, as regards England and Wales, to subdivide the subject chronologically into (1) the Ancient British Period; (2) the Anglo-Saxon Period; and (3) the period intervening between the Norman Conquest and the reign of Henry VII.

In this reign, it is believed, the last trace of the Wolf in England disappeared, since history thereafter is silent on the subject. In Scotland and

Ireland, however, this was by no means the case, as, later on, we shall be able to show.

GEOLOGICAL EVIDENCE.

Owing to the great similarity which exists between the skeleton of a Wolf and that of a large Dog, such as would be used in the chase, it is very difficult to distinguish between them. Professor Owen, in his

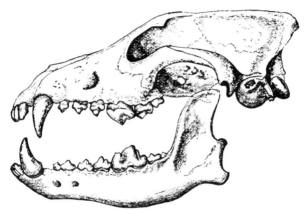

SKULL OF WOLF. ($\frac{1}{3}$ NAT. SIZE.)

"British Fossil Mammals," has remarked upon this difficulty, and, following Cuvier, has pointed out the chief distinguishing characters which may be relied upon for identification, and which lie chiefly in the skull. He says :—"The Wolf has the triangular part of the forehead behind the orbits a little narrower and flatter, the occipito-sagittal crest longer and loftier, and the teeth, especially the canines, proportionately larger."*

* Compare the crania of the Wolf here figured (pp. 120, 121) with those of the Dog, upper and under surfaces, given by Professor Flower in his "Osteology of the Mammalia," pp. 113, 116 (1st ed.).

So far as we have been enabled to collect the evidence, it would appear that undoubted remains of the Wolf have been found in the following localities, for a knowledge of many of which we are indebted to Professor Boyd Dawkins' able paper, "On the Distribution of the British Post-Glacial Mammals," published in the *Quarterly Journal* of the Geological Society, vol. xxv. 1869, p. 192.

BERKSHIRE.—Windsor (Mus. Geol. Survey).

DERBYSHIRE.—Pleasby Vale (Mus. Geol. Survey); Windy Knoll, Castleton (Dawkins, "Quart. Journ. Geol. Soc." xxxi. p. 246, and xxxiii. p. 727); Creswell Crag Caves (Mello and Busk, "Quart. Soc." xxxi. p. 684; Dawkins, op. cit. xxxii. p. 248, and xxxiii. pp. 590 and 602.)

DEVONSHIRE.—Bench Cave, Brixham (W. A. Sanford); Kent's Hole, Torquay (Mus. Geol. Soc., Mus Roy. Coll. Surg., and Mus. Oxford); Oreston, near Plymouth (Brit. Mus. and Mus. Geol. Soc.; Owen, "Brit. Foss. Mamm." p. 123).

GLAMORGANSHIRE.—Gower, Bacon's Hole (Mus. Swansea; Falconer, "Palæont. Mem." ii. pp. 183, 325, 340, 349, 501); Bosco's Hole (Mus. Swansea; Falconer, tom. cit. pp. 510, 589); Crow Hole (Mus. Swansea; Falconer, tom. cit. p. 519); Deborah Den (Mus. Swansea; Falconer, tom. cit. p. 467); Long Hole (Falconer, tom. cit. pp. 400, 525, 538); Minchin Hole (Brit. Mus.; Mus. Swansea); Paviland (Mus. Oxford and Swansea; Owen, "Brit. Foss. Mamm." p. 124); Ravenscliff (Falconer, tom. cit. p. 519); Spritsail Tor (id. pp. 179, 462, 477, 522).

GLOUCESTERSHIRE.—Tewkesbury (Owen, "Brit. Foss. Mamm.").

KENT.—Murston, Sittingbourne (Mus. Geol. Survey).

ESSEX.—Valley of the Roding, Ilford (Sir A. Brady).

NORFOLK.—Denver Sluice† (Mus. Geol. Cambr.).

OXFORDSHIRE.—Thame (Coll. Codrington, "Quart. Journ. Geol. Soc." xx. p. 374).

SOMERSETSHIRE.—Benwell Cave (W. Borrer); Blendon (Mus. Taunton); Hutton (Mus. Taunton); Sandford Hill (Mus. Taunton); Uphill (Mus. Bath and Taunton); Wokey Hole (Mus. Oxford, Taunton, and Bristol).

† A landscape by R. W. Fraser " On the Ouze near Denver Sluice " was exhibited at the Royal Academy in 1877, No. 794. The locality is a few miles to the South of Downham Market, and just below where the old and new Bedford rivers run into the natural stream.

SUSSEX.—Bracklesham (Brit. Mus. and Mus. Chichester); Peven-
sey* (" Sussex Archæol. Coll." xxiv. p. 160.)
WILTSHIRE.—Vale of Kennet (" Sussex Archæol." tom. cit.).
YORKSHIRE.—Bielbecks (Mus. York; " Phil. Mag." vol. vi. p. 225);
Kirkdale (Brit. Mus., Mus. Geol. Soc. and Roy. Coll. Surg;
Buckland, "Trans. Roy. Soc." 1822; Clift, id. 1823, p. 90).

We have here a dozen counties in different parts
of England and Wales, north, south, east, and west,
which show clearly from their position how very generally distributed the Wolf must formerly have been.

The geological record, however, is but an im-
perfect one in showing the distribution of the Wolf
in bygone times, for to the localities above mentioned
might be added numerous others in which we know
from history that this animal formerly abounded.
The forest of Riddlesdale in Northumberland ; the
great forests of Blackburnshire and Bowland in
Lancashire ; Richmond Forest, Yorkshire ; Sherwood
Forest, Nottinghamshire ; Savernake Forest, Wilts ;
the New Forest ; the forests of Bere and Irwell, and
many others, are on record as former strongholds of
these ferocious animals. To these we shall have
occasion to refer later when dealing with the
historical evidence.

Unlike other extinct British animals, the Wolf
apparently has not deteriorated in size, for the fossil
bones which have been discovered, as above mentioned, are not larger, nor in any way to be distinguished from those of European wolves of the
present day.

* In 1851 many skulls of Wolves were taken out of a disused
mediæval well at Pevensey Castle.

Ancient British Period. — Dio Nicæus, speaking of the inhabitants of the northern parts of this island, tells us they were a fierce and barbarous

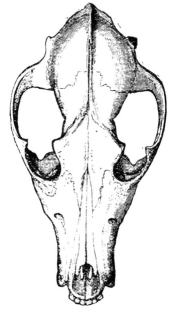

CRANIUM OF WOLF.   UPPER SURFACE.   ($\frac{1}{3}$ NAT. SIZE.)

people, who tilled no ground, but lived upon the depredations they committed in the southern districts or upon the food they procured by hunting. Strabo also says (lib. iv.) that the dogs bred in Britain were highly esteemed upon the Continent on account of their excellent qualities for hunting, and these qualities, he seems to hint, were natural to

6

them, and not the effect of tutorage by their foreign masters. Wolf-hunting appears to have been a favourite pursuit with the ancient Britons. Mempricius or Memprys, one of the immediate descendants of Brutus, who reigned until B.C. 980, fell a victim

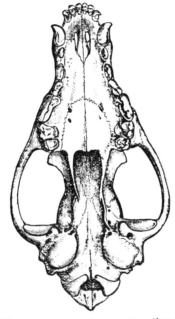

CRANIUM OF WOLF. UNDER SURFACE. ($\frac{1}{3}$ NAT. SIZE.)

in that year to the Wolves which he delighted to pursue, and was unfortunately devoured by them.

> "Hys brothir he slwe—
> For tyl succede tyl hym as kyng.
> It happynde syne at a huntyng
> Wytht wolwys hym to weryde be ;
> Swa endyit his iniquite."
> *Wyntownis Cronykil*, i. p. 54.

Blaiddyd, another British monarch (B.C. 863), who seems to have been learned in chemistry, is said to have discovered the medicinal properties of the Bath mineral waters, by observing that cattle when attacked and wounded by the Wolves went and stood in these waters, and were then healed much sooner then they would have been by any other means. From this it may be inferred that Wolf-hunting was found by the ancient Britons to be a necessary and pleasurable, yet dangerous, pursuit.

We do not find, says Strutt,[*] that during the establishment of the Romans in Britain, there were any restrictive laws promulgated respecting the killing of game. It appears to have been an established maxim in the early jurisprudence of that people, to invest the right of such things as had no master with those who were the first possessors. Wild beasts, birds, and fishes became the property of those who first could take them. It is most probable that the Britons were left at liberty to exercise their ancient privileges; for had any severity been exerted to prevent the destruction of game, such laws would hardly have been passed over without the slightest notice being taken of them by the ancient historians.

Anglo-Saxon Period.—As early as the ninth century, and doubtless long before that, a knowledge of hunting formed an essential part of the education of a young nobleman. Asser, in his " Life of Alfred the Great," assures us that that monarch before he was twelve years of age " was a most expert and active hunter, and excelled in all the branches of that most

* " Sports and Pastimes of the People of England."

8

noble art, to which he applied with incessant labour and amazing success." Hunting the Wolf, the Wild Boar, the Fox, and the Deer, were the favourite pastimes of the nobility of that day, and the Dogs which they employed for these various branches of the sport, were held by them in the highest estimation.

Such ravages did the Wolves commit during winter,

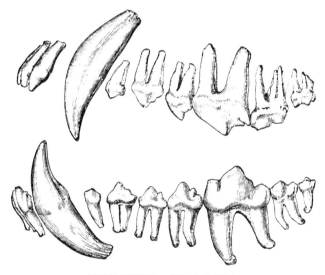

TEETH OF WOLF. NATURAL SIZE.

particularly in January when the cold was severest, that the Saxons distinguished that month by the name of "Wolf month."

"The month which we now call January," says Verstegan, "they called 'Wolf monat,' to wit, 'Wolf moneth,' because people are wont always in that month to be in more danger to be devoured of Wolves than in any season else of the year; for that, through the extremity of cold and snow, these ravenous

9

creatures could not find of other beasts sufficient to feed upon."*

The Saxons also called an outlaw "wolfs-head,"† as being out of the protection of the law, proscribed, and as liable to be killed as that destructive beast. "*Et tunc gerunt caput lupinum, ita quod sine judiciali inquisitione rite pereant.*"‡

In the "Penitentiale" of Archbishop Egbert, drawn up about A.D. 750, it is laid down (lib. iv.) that, "if a wolf shall attack cattle of any kind, and the animal attacked shall die in consequence, no Christian may touch it."

It is to the terror which the Wolf inspired among our forefathers that we are to ascribe the fact of kings and rulers, in a barbarous age, feeling proud of bearing the name of this animal as an attribute of courage and ferocity. Brute power was then considered the highest distinction of man, and the sentiment was not mitigated by those refinements of modern life which conceal but do not destroy it. We thus find, amongst our Anglo-Saxon kings and great men, such names as Ethelwulf, "the Noble Wolf;" Berthwulf, "the Illustrious Wolf;" Eadwulf, "the Prosperous Wolf;" Ealdwulf, "the Old Wolf."

In Athelstan's reign, Wolves abounded so in Yorkshire that a retreat was built by one Acehorn, at

* "Restitution of Decayed Intelligence," p. 64 (ed. 1673).

† Ang.-Sax. *Wulvesheofod*, that is, having the head of a Wolf. In 1041, the fugitive Godwin was proclaimed *Wulvesheofod*, a price being set upon his head. The term was in use temp. Henry II.

‡ Bracton, "De legibus et consuetudinibus Angliæ," lib. iii. tr. ii. c. 11 (1569). *See* also Knighton, "De Eventibus Angliæ," in Twysden's "Historiæ Angiicanæ Scriptores Decem," p. 2356 (1652).

Flixton, near Filey, in that county, wherein travellers might seek refuge if attacked by them.

Camden says :—" More inward stands Flixton, where a hospital was built in the time of Athelstan, for defending travellers from Wolves (as it is word for word in the public records), that they should not be devoured by them."* It is currently believed that a farmhouse between the villages of Flixton and Staxton now stands on the site of this hospital. It was restored and confirmed in 1447 by the name of Canons Spittle, and was dissolved about 1535. The farm is still called Spittal Farm, and a small stream running by it is called Spittal Brook.†

When Athelstan, in 938, obtained a signal victory at Brunanburgh over Constantine, King of Wales, he imposed upon him a yearly tribute of money and cattle, to which was also added a certain number of "hawks and sharp-scented dogs, fit for the hunting of wild beasts."‡ His successor, Edgar, remitted the pecuniary payment on condition of receiving annually from Ludwall§ (or Idwal‖), the successor of Constantine, the skins of three hundred Wolves.¶

* Camden, "Britannia," tit. Yorkshire, vol. ii. p. 902.

† This information was communicated to the author by the Rev. Henry Blane, of Folkton Rectory, Ganton, York.

‡ William of Malmesbury, "Hist. Reg. Anglorum," lib. ii. c. 6.

§ Cf. Holinshed's "Chronicles," vol. i. p. 378 (4to ed. 1807), and Selden's Notes to Drayton's "Polyolbion," Song ix.

‖ Cf. Camden's "Britannia," tit. Merionethshire, vol. ii. p. 785.

¶ William of Malmesbury, op. cit. lib. ii. c. 8. See also the quaint remarks on this subject by Taylor, the Water Poet, in his "Journey through Wales," 1652 (pp. 31, 32, Halliwell's edition, 1859). The value of a wolf-skin in Wales, as fixed by the Code of Laws made by Howel Dha in the ninth century, was eightpence, the same value being set upon an otter-skin.

We do not find, indeed, that the hawks and hounds were included in this new stipulation, but it does not seem reasonable that Edgar, who, like his predecessor, was extremely fond of field sports, should have remitted that part of the tribute.*

It is generally admitted that Edgar relinquished the fine of gold and silver imposed by his uncle Athelstan upon Constantine, and claimed in its stead the annual production of 300 wolf-skins, because, say the historians, the extensive woodlands and coverts, abounding at that time in Britain, afforded shelter for the Wolves, which were exceedingly numerous, especially in the districts bordering upon Wales. By this prudent expedient, in less than four years, it is said, the whole island was cleared of these ferocious animals, without putting his subjects to the least expense.† But, as Strutt has observed,‡ "if this record be taken in its full latitude, and the supposition established, that the Wolves were totally exterminated in Britain during the reign of Edgar, more will certainly be admitted than is consistent with the truth, as certain documents clearly prove." The words of William of Malmesbury on the subject are to this effect, that "he, Edgar, imposed a tribute upon the King of Wales, exacting yearly 300 Wolves. This tribute

* Strutt, "Sports and Pastimes."

† It is singular that the same expedient has been resorted to in modern times, and with considerable success. In the accounts of Assinniboia, Red River Territory, there is an entry of payment for Wolves' heads; and in 1868 the State of Minnesota paid for Wolves' scalps 11,300 dollars, at the rate of 10 dollars apiece.

‡ "Sports and Pastimes."

continued to be paid for three years, but ceased upon the fourth, because, '*nullum se ulterius posse invenire professus*,' it was said that he could not find any more."*

"Cambria's proud Kings (tho' with reluctance) paid
  Their tributary wolves; head after head,
  In full account, till the woods yield no more,
  And all the rav'nous race extinct is lost."
SOMERVILE'S *Chace*.

But this must be taken to refer only to Wales, for in the first place it can hardly be supposed that the Welsh chieftain would be permitted to hunt out of his own dominions, and in the next place there is abundant documentary evidence to prove the existence of Wolves in England for many centuries later.

Holinshed, who gives a much fuller account, says :†—"The happie and fortunate want of these beasts in England is vniuersallie ascribed to the politike government of King Edgar, who to the intent the whole countrie might once be clensed and clearelie rid of them, charged the conquered Welshmen (who were then pestered with these rauenous creatures aboue measure) to paie him a yearlie tribute of woolfes skinnes, to be gathered within the land. He appointed them thereto a certaine number of 300, with free libertie for their prince to hunt and pursue them ouer all quarters of the realme ; as our chronicles doo report. Some there be which write

* "Hist. Reg. Anglorum," lib. ii. cap. 8. *See* also Wynne's "Caradoc," p. 51.
† "Chronicles of England, Scotland, and Ireland" (ed. 4to, 1807), vol. i. p. 378, bk. iii. chap. iv.: 'Of Savage Beasts and Vermines.'

how Ludwall, prince of Wales, paid yearelie to King Edgar this tribute of 300 woolfes, whose carcases being brought into Lloegres, were buried at Wolfpit, in Cambridgeshire, and that by meanes thereof within the compasse and terme of foure yeares, none of these noisome creatures were left to be heard of within Wales and England. Since this time, also, we read not that anie woolfe hath beene seene here that hath beene bred within the bounds and limits of our countrie : howbeit there haue beene diuerse brought over from beyond the seas for greedinesse of gaine, and to make monie onlie by the gasing and gaping of our people vpon them, who couet oft to see them, being strange beasts in their eies, and sildome knowne (as I haue said) in England."

This event is related somewhat differently by the Welsh historians. " In the year 965," says Powel, " the country of North Wales was cruelly wasted by the army of Edgar, King of England ; the occasion of which was, the non-payment of the tribute that the king of Aberffraw (North Wales), by the laws of Howel Dha, was obliged to pay to the king of London (England). But at length a peace was concluded upon these conditions, that the king of North Wales, instead of money, should pay to the king of England the tribute of 300 Wolves yearly ; which creature was then very pernicious and destructive to England and Wales. This tribute being duly performed for two years, the third year there were none to be found in any part of the island, so that afterwards the prince of North Wales became exempt

14

from paying any acknowledgment to the king of England."

The amount of the original tribute commuted for this tax of Wolves, the time when that tribute was appointed, and the cause for which it was imposed, are altogether circumstances not very generally understood. It is vaguely imagined to have been a degrading tax paid by the people of Wales to the English monarch, in token of their subjection to his sovereignty as their conqueror. "This," says Powel, "is not the fact; it arose from a local cause: from one of those cruel dissensions among the native princes which too often disgrace the Welsh annals, and to settle which the weakest never failed to invite the aid of foreign force.

About the year 953, Owen, the son of Griffith, was slain by the men of Cardigan; and Athelstane, upon this pretext, entering with an army into Wales, imposed an annual tribute upon certain princes to the amount of £20 in gold, £300 in silver, and 200 head of cattle, but which was not observed by these Welsh princes, as appears by the laws of Howel Dha, wherein the levy is appointed. It is there decreed that the Prince of Aberffraw should pay no more to the English king than £66 tribute, and even this sum was to be contributed to the prince of Aberffraw by the princes of Dinefawr and Powis, upon whom this tax was virtually imposed. The principality of Dinefawr, it may be observed, included Cardigan, by the men of which district the alleged crime had been committed; and Powis, which was close to the

English borders, was apparently implicated in the same offence."

Hence it appears the tax was a local fine imposed upon these two princes, only that the prince of North Wales was made answerable for its due performance. The tax existed therefore, though but nominally, for the space of two-and-thirty years—namely, from the time of Athelstane to Edgar—when the above recorded commutation of the tribute took place, and for the fulfilment of which condition it is apparent the prince of North Wales was again made answerable.

That the principality of Wales was, by this salutary means, delivered in a great measure from the pest of Wolves may be conceived. In this the histories of the Welsh agree; but there is some shade of difference in their conclusions as to the utter extermination of the race; and it is now believed that they were not entirely destroyed in Wales till years after. Owen, in his " Cambrian Biography," says it was not till forty-five years after.*

Drayton, in his " Polyolbion" (Song ix.), has thus commemorated the wisdom of Edgar's policy :—

> " Thrice famous Saxon king, on whom Time ne'er shall prey.
> O Edgar! who compell'dst our Ludwall hence to pay
> Three hundred Wolves a year for tribute unto thee;
> And for that tribute paid, as famous may'st thou be,
> O conquer'd British king, by whom was first destroy'd
> The multitude of Wolves that long this land annoy'd."

* "Iago ap Idwal Voel, king of Gwynedd, from A.D. 948 to 979. From 948 to 966 he reigned jointly with his brother Jevav. In 962 Edgar made him pay tribute of wolves' heads; and in forty-five years after, all these animals were destroyed."

The learned Dr. Kay* acquiesced in the vulgar opinion of the extinction of Wolves in England by King Edgar, and in his work on "British Dogs," published in 1570, treating of the sheep-dog (*Pastoralis*) he says: "*Sunt qui scribunt Ludwallum Cambriæ principem pendisse annuatim Edgaro regi 300 luporum tributi nomine, atque ita annis quatuor omnem Cambriam, atque adeo omnem Angliam, orbasse lupis.*"

"*Regnavit autem Edgarus circiter annum 959, a quo tempore non legimus nativum in Anglia visum lupum.*"

The worthy doctor seems to have been little aware that even at the date at which he wrote wolves still existed in the British Islands. Dr. John Walker was almost as much at fault when he wrote: "*Canis lupus. Habitavit olim in Britannia. Quondam incola sylvæ caledoniæ. In Scotia seculo xv. extinctus, et postremo in regione Naverniæ.*"†

Pennant, referring to the received opinion that a great part of the kingdom was freed from Wolves through the exertions of King Edgar, says:—" In England he attempted to effect it by commuting the punishments for certain crimes into the acceptance of a number of Wolves' tongues from each criminal; in Wales by converting a tax of gold and silver into an annual tribute of 300 Wolves' heads. Notwithstanding his endeavours, however, and the assertions

* "Joannis Caii Britanni ' de Canibus Britannicis.' " Liber unus. Londini, per Gulielmum Seresium. 8vo, 1570. There is a translation of this work in the British Museum, entitled, " Of Englishe Dogges, newly drawn into English." By Abraham Fleming, Student. London. 4to, 1576. A reprint of this has been recently published.

† ' Mammalia Scotica,' in " Essays on Nat. Hist. and Rural Economy," 1814, p. 480.

17

of some authors to the contrary, his scheme proved abortive."*

We have met with a statement to the effect that "two wooden Wolves' heads still remain near Glastonbury on an ancient house where [query, on the site of which] at Eadgerly, King Edgar lived and received annually his tax from the Welsh in 300 heads."†

This statement, however, conflicts somewhat with that of Holinshed, who says that " the carcases being brought into Lloegres, were buried at Wolfpit in Cambridgeshire."‡

In the Forest Laws of Canute, promulgated in 1016, the Wolf is thus expressly mentioned :—" As for foxes and wolves, they are neither reckoned as beasts of the forest or of venery, and therefore whoever kills any of them is out of all danger of forfeiture, or making any recompense or amends for the same. Nevertheless, the killing them within the limits of the forest is a breach of the royal chase, and therefore the offender shall yield a recompense for the same, though it be but easy and gentle."§

It was doubtless to this constitution that the Solicitor-General St. John referred, at the trial of the Earl of Strafford, when he said, " We give law to hares and deer, because they are beasts of chase ; but we give no law to wolves and foxes, because they are

---

* " British Zoology," vol. i. p. 88 (1812).
† " Sussex Archæol. Coll." vol. iv. p. 83 (1851).
‡ " Chronicles," vol. i. p. 378 (4to ed. 1807).
§ *See* Manwood's " Forest Laws." The Charter of the Forest of Canutus the Dane (§ 27).

beasts of prey, but knock them on the head wherever we find them."*

Liulphus, a dean of Whalley in the time of Canute, was celebrated as a wolf-hunter at Rossendale, Lancashire.†

Matthew Paris, in his "Lives of the Abbots of St. Albans," mentions a grant of church lands by Abbot Leofstan (the 12th abbot of that monastery) to Thurnoth and others, in consideration of their keeping the woods between the Chiltern Hundreds and London free from wolves and other wild beasts.

It would seem that the "ancient and accustomed tribute" due to the English kings was repeated by the Welsh princes in the very last years of the Anglo-Saxon monarchy. It was demanded by and rendered to Harold.‡

Period from the Conquest to the reign of Henry VII. —Historical evidence of the existence of wolves in Great Britain before the Norman Conquest, as might be expected, is meagre and unsatisfactory, and the abundance of these animals in our islands prior to that date is chiefly to be inferred from the measures which in later times were devised for their destruction.

In the "Carmen de Bello Hastingensi," by Guido, Bishop of Amiens (v. 571), it is related that William the Conqueror left the dead bodies of the English upon the battle-field to be devoured by worms, wolves, birds, and dogs—*vermibus, atque lupis, avibus, cani-*

* Clarendon, "Hist. Reb." fol. ed., i. p. 183.
† Whitaker's "History of Whalley," p. 222. ‡ Palgrave.

busque voranda. When Waltheof, the son of Siward, with an invading Danish army arrived in the Humber, in September, 1069, and, reinforced by the men of Northumbria, made an attack upon York, it is related that 3,000 Normans fell. A hundred of the chiefest in rank were said to have fallen amongst the flames by the hand of Waltheof himself, and the Scalds of the North sang how the son of Siward gave the corpses of the Frenchmen as a choice banquet for the Wolves of Northumberland.*

In 1076 Robert de Umfraville,† Knight, lord of Toures and Tain, otherwise called "Robert with the Beard," being kinsman to that king, obtained from him a grant of the lordship, valley, and forest of Riddesdale, in the county of Northumberland, with all castles, manors, lands, woods, pastures, waters, pools, and royal franchises which were formerly possessed by Mildred, the son of Akman, late lord of Riddesdale, and which came to that king upon his conquest of England; to hold by the service of defending that part of the country for ever from enemies *and Wolves*, with the sword which King William had by his side when he entered Northumberland.‡

1087–1100. The inveterate love of the chase

---

* Freeman's "Norman Conquest."

† "The name seems to be derived from one of the several places in Normandy now called Amfreville, but in some instances originally Omfreville, that is *Humfredi villa*, the vill or abode of Humphrey." —Lower, *Patronymica Britannica.*

‡ See Dugdale's "Baronage," vol. i. p. 504; and Blount's "Ancient Tenures," p. 241.

possessed by William Rufus, which prompted him to enforce, during his tragical reign, the most stringent and cruel forest laws, is too well known to readers of history to require comment. It cannot be doubted that in the vast forests* which then covered the greater part of the country, and through which he continuously hunted, he must have encountered and slain many a Wolf. Yet, strange to say, a careful search through a great number of volumes has resulted in a failure to discover any evidence upon this point, or indeed any mention of the Wolf in connection with this monarch.

Longstaffe, in his account of " Durham before the Conquest," states that a great increase of Wolves took place in Richmondshire during this century, and mentions incidentally that Richard Ingeniator dealing with property at Wolverston (called Olveston in the time of William Rufus) sealed the grant with an impression of a Wolf.

1100-1135. In his passion for hunting wild animals, Henry I. excelled even his brother William, and not content with encountering and slaying those which, like the Wolf and the Wild-boar, were at that time indigenous to this country, he " cherished of set purpose sundrie kinds of wild beasts, as bears, libards, ounces, lions, at Woodstocke and one or two other places in England, which he walled about with

* " The word 'forest,' in its original and most extended sense, implied a tract of land lying out (*foras*), that is, rejected, as of no value, in the first distribution of property."—WHITAKER, *History of Whalley*, p. 193.

hard stone An. 1120, and where he would often fight with some one of them hand to hand."*

Amongst other forest laws made in this reign, was one which provided that compensation should be made for any injury occasioned during a wolf hunt. *Si quis arcu vel balista de subitanti, vel pedico ad lupos vel ad aliud capiendum posito, dampanum vel malum aliquod recipiat, solvat qui posuit.*†

1156. There can be no doubt that at this period, and for some time afterwards, the New Forest, as well as the Forest of Bere, in Hampshire, both favourite hunting-grounds with William Rufus and his brother Henry, were the strongholds of the Wolf. as they were of the Wild-boar and the Red-deer, for in the second year of the reign of Henry II. the sheriff of Hants had an allowance made to him in the Exchequer for several sums by him disbursed for the livery of the King's *wolf-hunters*, hawkers, falconers, and others. " *Et in liberatione lupariorum* 100s., *et in liberatione accipitrariorum et falconariorum Regis* 22*li per Willelmum Cumin.*"‡

In the fourth year of the same reign, the sheriffs of London were allowed by the Chancellor 40s. out of the Exchequer for the King's huntsmen and his dogs. " *Et venatorilus Regis et canibus ejus* xl*s. per cancellarium.*"§

Conan, Duke of Brittany and Earl of Richmond,

* Harrison's "Description of England," prefixed to Holinshed's "Chronicle," p. 226.

† "Leges Regis Henrici primi," cap. 90, § 2.

‡ Madox, "History and Antiquities of the Exchequer of the Kings of England from the Norman Conquest to the end of the Reign of Edward II.," vol. i. p. 204 (1769).

§ Madox, tom. cit. p. 207.

in 1164, granted, amongst other privileges, to the Abbey of Jourvaulx, several pastures on the north side of the river Jore, reserving only liberty for his deer, likewise pasturage throughout his new forest, near Richmond, Yorkshire, for all their cattle, with power to keep hounds for chasing Wolves out of those their territories.*

It is related in the "Annales Cambriæ" (Harl. MSS., No. 3859 on vellum) that in 1166 a rabid Wolf at Caermarthen bit twenty-two persons, nearly all of whom died.†

In 1167, the Bishopric of Hereford was vested in the King in consequence of the see being then vacant; and in the account of John Cumin, who acted in the capacity of Custos, we find in the accounts of the revenue and expenditure of the temporalities a payment of 10s. for three Wolves captured that year. "*Et pro tribus Lupis capiendis, x*.*"

William Beriwere obtained from Henry II. the confirmation of all his lands, as also the forestership of the Forest of De la Bere, with power to take any person transgressing therein between the bars of Hampton and the gates of Winchester, and likewise between the river of Ramsey and the river of Winchester to the sea, as amply as his father had held the same in the times of King William and King Henry I. From Richard I. (whom he accompanied

* Dugdale's "Baronage," vol. i. p. 48. "Ex. Regist. Archiep. Cant." p. 875a.

† "*Apud Kermerden lupus rabiosus duo de viginto homines momordit qui omnes fere protinus perierunt.*" This MS. is believed to be a translation from the original Welsh. Ed. Williams (Master of the Rolls Series), pp. 50, 51.

to the Holy Land, and whom he was instrumental in delivering from prison when that king was confined in Germany) he obtained many valuable emoluments as well as large territorial grants, and in the following reign was no less fortunate with King John, who, having a great regard for him in consequence of his knowledge in the art and mystery of venery, gave him license to enclose his woods at Joare, Cadelegh, Raddon, Ailesberie, and Burgh Walter, with free liberty to hunt the hare, fox, cat, and *Wolf*, throughout all Devonshire, and likewise the goat beyond the precincts of the forest; and to have free warren throughout all his own lands for hares, pheasants, and partridges.*

From a charter of liberties granted by King John, when Earl of Morton, to the inhabitants of Devonshire, it appears that the Wolf was at that time included amongst the " beasts of venery " in that county. The original deed, which is still preserved in the custody of the Dean and Chapter of Exeter, is under seal, and provides *inter alia* as follows :—

" *Quod habeant canes suos et alias libertates, sicut melius et liberius illas haberunt tempore ejusd. Henrici regis et reisellos suos, et quod capiant capreolum, vulpem, cattum, lupum, leporem, lutram, ubicumque illa invenirent extra regardum forestæ meæ.*"†

1209. Mr. Evelyn P. Shirley has printed ‡ two

---

* Dugdale's " Baronage," vol. i. p. 701.

† Ex Autographo penes Dec. et Capit. Exon. From Bp. Lyttelton's Collection. Quoted by Pennant, " British Zoology," vol. ii. p. 308.

‡ " Collectanea Topographica et Genealogica," vol. vi. p. 299.

deeds of the 10th of John relating to the manor of Henwick, in the parish of Bulwick, county Northampton, held by the tenure of hunting the Wolf (*fugaco'm lupi*), and he suggests that from this tenure probably the family of Luvet or Lovett, originally of Rushton, and afterwards of Astwell, in the county of Northampton, bore, for their arms : Argent, three Wolves, passant, in pale, sable, armed and langued, gules.*

1212. In this year, when the neighbourhood around Kingsclere was all forest, an entry occurs in the Patent Rolls of a payment of 5*s.* as a reward for the capture of a Wolf at Freemantle.† The Roll referred to is doubtless the *Rotulus Misæ, annis Regis Johannis quartodecimi* (1212–1213), where the following entries occur relating to the capture or chase of the Wolf:—

" On Thursday next in the octave of the Holy Trinity [May 12], for a Wolf captured at Freemantle, [Surrey] by the dogs of Master Ernald de Auclent, 5*s.*"

" *Item.* [at Hereford]. Thursday next following the Feast of St. Martin [Nov. 22] to Norman the keeper of the Veltrars,‡ and to Wilkin Doggett, his associate, for two Wolves captured in the forest of Irwell, 10*s.*, by the king's command, &c."

" *Item.* Wednesday next following the Feast of

* The Wolf frequently appears on heraldic bearings.
† " Patent Rolls," May 31, 1212, quoted in " Sussex Archæological Collections," xxiv. p. 161.
‡ *Veltrarius,* or *vautrarius,* from the French *vaultre,* was a mongrel hound for the chase of the wild-boar. See Blount, " Ancient Tenures," p. 233.

St. Gregory [March 12], for two Wolves captured, one at Boscha de Furchiis, the other at Willes, 10s., given to Smalobbe and Wilck, the keepers of the veltrariõ of Thomas de Sandford."

It is perhaps not generally known that the circumstance narrated in the story of Bedd Gêlert, with which every one is familiar, is said to have occurred in the reign of King John, and, as it is a story of a British Wolf, it is scarcely to be passed over here without some brief notice, the more so as it is not at all unlikely that it is founded on fact.

The tradition, as related by Bingley in his "Tour round North Wales,"* is to the effect that Llewellyn, who was Prince of Wales in the reign of King John, resided at the foot of Snowdon, and, amongst a number of other hounds which he possessed, had one of rare excellence which had been given to him by the king. On one occasion, during the absence of the family, a Wolf entered the house; and Llewellyn, who first returned, was met at the door by his favourite dog, who came out, covered with blood, to greet his master. The prince, alarmed, ran into the house, to find his child's cradle overturned, and the ground flowing with blood. In a moment of terror, imagining that the dog had killed the child, he plunged his sword into his body, and laid him dead on the spot. But, on turning up the cradle, he found his boy alive and sleeping by the side of the dead Wolf. This circumstance had such an effect on

* "A Tour round North Wales," 1800, vol. i. p. 363. See also Sir John Carr's "Stranger in Ireland," 4to, 1806.

the mind of the prince, that he erected a tomb over the faithful dog's grave on the spot where afterwards the parish church was built, called from this incident Bedd Gêlert, or the grave of Gêlert. From this story was derived the common Welsh proverb, "I repent as much as the man who slew his greyhound."

The dog referred to belonged probably to the race called by Pennant "the Highland gre-hound," of great size and strength, deep-chested, and covered with long rough hair. This kind was much esteemed in former days, and was used for hunting by all the great chieftains in preference to any other. Boethius styles it "*genus venaticum cum celerrimum tum audacissimum.*"

1216–1272. In the following reign of Henry III. Wolves were sufficiently numerous in some parts of the country to induce the king to make grants of land to various individuals upon the express condition of their taking measures to destroy these animals wherever they could be found.

In 1242 it appears that Vitalis Engaine made partition with William de Cantelupe, Baron of Bergavenny, of the manor of Badmundesfield, in Suffolk, as heir to William de Curtenai, and the same year had a summons, amongst divers great men, to attend the king, well appointed with horse and arms, in his expedition into France. He died in 1249, seized, *inter alia*, of part of the lordships of Laxton and Pichesle, in the county of Northampton, held by "petit serjeanty"—viz., *to hunt the Wolf whensoever the king should command.**

* Dugdale's "Baronage," vol. i. p. 466.

Selden, in his notes to Drayton's "Polyolbion" (ix. 76), refers to the manor of Piddlesey in Leicestershire, which was held by one Henry of Angage *per serjeantiam capiendi lupos,* and quotes as his authority "Itin. Leicesters. 27 Hen. III. in Archiv. Turr. Lond." In the same reign, William de Limeres held of the king, *in capite,* in the county of Southampton, one carucate* of land in Comelessend by the service of hunting the Wolf with the king's dogs.†

1272–1307. In the third year of the reign of Edward I., namely, in 1275, Sir John d'Engayne, knight, and Elena d'Engayne, his wife, held lands in Pightesley, in the county of Northampton, by the service of hunting the Wolf, *for his pleasure,* in that county,‡ from which it is to be inferred that this animal was then common enough to be hunted for sport, as the fox is now-a-days. Other lands in the same county were held at this time on condition of the tenant finding dogs "for the destruction of Wolves" and other animals.§ It appears by the Patent Rolls of the 9th year of Edward I. that in 1280, John Giffard of Brymmesfield or Brampfield, was empowered to destroy the Wolves in all the king's forests throughout the realm. ‖

In 1281, Peter Corbet was commissioned to destroy

* Carucate, a plough land. As much arable land as one plough, with the animals that worked it, could cultivate in a year.
† Esc. temp. H. R. fil. R. Johannis. Harl. MS. Brit. Mus. No. 708, p. 8.
‡ Plac. Coron. 3 Edw. I. Rot. 20, *dorso.* Blount, "Ancient Tenures," p. 230.
§ Camden, "Britannia," p. 525, and Blount, p. 257.
‖ "Calend. Rot. Pat.," 49. See also Rymer's "Fœdera," *sub anno.*

all the Wolves he could find in the counties of Gloucester, Worcester, Hereford, Salop, and Stafford, and the bailiffs in the several counties were directed to be ready and assist him. The commission, which has been frequently referred to by different writers, runs as follows :—

" Pro Petro Corbet, de lupis capiendis.

" Rex, omnibus Ballivis, &c. Sciatis quod injunximus delecto et fideli nostro Petro Corbet quod in omnibus forestis et parcis et aliis locis intra comitatus nostros Gloucester, Wygorn, Hereford, Salop, et Stafford, in quibus *lupi* poterunt inveniri, *lupos* cum hominibus canibus et ingeniis suis capiat et destruat modis omnibus quibus viderit expedire.

" Et ideo vobis mandamus quod idem intendentes et auxiliantes estis.

" Teste rege apud Westm. 14 Maii A.D. 1281.'"*

In the Wardrobe Accounts of Edward I. preserved in the British Museum (Add. MS. No. 7966) anno 29 Edw. I. (1301), the following entry occurs :—

"April 29. To the huntsman of Sir Peter Corbet, deceased, for bringing to the King the dogs which belonged to the said Peter at the time of his death . . . . 6s. 8d.

In 1285, William de Reynes held two carucates† of land at Boyton, in the parish of Finchingfield, in the county of Essex, by the serjeanty of keeping for the king five Wolf-dogs (*canes luporarios*).‡ In the

* Rymer's " Fœdera," i. pt. 2, p. 192; ii. p. 168.
† See note on last page.
‡ Plac. Coron. 13 Edw. I. Essex; Blount, " Ancient Tenures," p. 236.

29

following year, John Engaine was returned as hold-
ing one carucate of land in Great Gidding, in the
county of Huntingdon, by the serjeanty of hunting
the Wolf, fox, and wild cat, and driving away all
vermin out of the forest of the king in that county.*
About the same time, Richard Engaine held one
hundred shillings of land in the town of Guedding, in
the county of Cambridge, by the serjeanty of taking
Wolves, and he was to do this service *daily* (*et
facit servit suum cotidie*),† from which it may be
inferred that Wolves at this date were particularly
troublesome. Indeed, it is recorded that during this
reign in a certain park at Farley the deer were
entirely destroyed by Wolves.‡

In 1297 John Engaine died, seized, *inter alia*, of
certain lands in Pytesle, Northampton, found to be
held of the king by the service of hunting the Wolf, fox
[cat], badger [wild boar, and hare] ; and likewise the
manor of Great Gidding in com. Huntendon, held by
the service of catching the hare, fox, cat, and Wolf
within the counties of Huntendon, Northampton,
Buckingham, and Roteland.§

In the accounts of Bolton Priory, quoted in
Whitaker's "History of Craven" (p. 331), occur
entries in the years 1306–1307, of payments made in

* "Plac. Coron. 14 Edw. I. Rot. 7," *dorso;* Blount, p. 230.
† "Testa de Nevil," p. 358; Blount, p. 262.
‡ "Will. Poer fecit parcum apud Farley et quod pater Comitis
Gilberti de Clare comes Gloucestriæ dedit ei quasdam feras ad præ-
dictum parcum instaurandum, quæ feræ per lupos destruebantur."
18 Edw. I. (1290) Wygorn. rot. 50 in abbreviat. Rotul.
§ Dugdale's "Baronage," vol. i. p. 466. See also the *Rotuli
Hundredorum,* ii. p. 627.

reward for the slaughter of Wolves, as " *Cuidam qui occidit lupum,*" but the price paid to the slayer is not stated. Whitaker in a note to this remarks:— " Wolves, therefore, though rare, were not extinct in Craven in the beginning of the fourteenth century. This is an important circumstance."

1307-1327. In the fourth year of Edward II. (1311) a composition was made between Sir John de Mowbray, son and heir of Sir Roger de Mowbray, of the one part, and the Abbot of Selby of the other part, whereby the said Sir John quitclaimed and released to the abbot all his right in the soil and manor of Crowle and other places therein mentioned, and the abbot and convent granted to the said Sir John de Mowbray certain woods, saving their free warren of goats, foxes, Wolves, conies, &c.*

The king's forest of the Peak in Derbyshire was of great extent, and about this time was much infested with Wolves. A family of the hereditary name of Wolfhunt held lands by the service of keeping the forest clear of these destructive animals.† From the records in the Tower of London (13 Edw. II.) it appears that in 1320 some persons held lands at Wormhill, in the county of Derby, by the service of hunting and taking Wolves, from whence they were called Wolfhunt or Wolvehunt.

Mr. W. H. G. Bagshawe, of Ford Hall, Chapel-en-

* Burton, " Monasticon Eboracense," p. 389. The Abbots of Selby and of St. Mary, at York, were the only two mitred abbots in Yorkshire.

† 'The Local Laws, Courts, and Customs of Derbyshire,' " Journ. Brit. Archæol. Assoc." vol. vii. p. 197.

le-Frith, Derbyshire, a descendant of the same family as Mr. F. W. Bagshawe, the present owner of Worm-hill Hall, in reply to inquiries on the subject, has been good enough to write as follows :—

"With the particulars in Blount's 'Tenures' I have long been familiar, but I am sorry to say that I cannot add to them. Wormhill Hall was never, so far as I know, held under the tenure of destroying Wolves, but it is most probable that a portion of the lands there were originally held by the tenure of preserving the king's 'verte and venyson' in his forest of the Peak. There is a tradition that the last Wolf in England was killed at Wormhill, but I never saw any evidence of it, nor did I ever hear any date assigned. In my pedigree of our family I find a note to the effect that John de l'Hall (the ancestor of John de l'Hall, whose daughter Alice was the wife of Nicholas Bagshawe) was appointed a forester (of fee, I suppose) to the king by deed dated 1349."*

In 1321 William Michell, son and heir of John Michell, held a messuage and land at Middelton Lillebon, co. Wilts, of the king *in capite*, by the serjeanty of keeping his Wolf-dogs—*per serjantiam custodiendi canes luparios Regis.*†

1327–1377. So far as can be gathered from history, it would seem that while stringent measures were being devised for the destruction of Wolves in all or most of the inhabited districts which they frequented,

* Camden, "Britannia," tit. Derbyshire, i. p. 591 ; Blount, "Ancient Tenures," p. 250.

† *Luparios* elsewhere *luporarios*: Harl. MS. Brit. Mus. No. 134, p. 80. Blount, "Ancient Tenures," p. 258.

in the less populous and more remote parts of the country, steps were taken by such of the principal landowners as were fond of hunting to secure their own participation in the sport of finding and killing them.

In Edward III.'s time, Conan, Duke of Brittany, in 1342, gave pasture for cattle through all his new forest at Richmond in Yorkshire to the inmates of the Abbey of Fors in Wensleydale, forbidding them to use any mastiffs to drive the Wolves from their pastures.*

In the same year, Alan, Earl of Brittany, gave them common of pasture through all his forest of " Wandesley-dale ;" and to cut as much grass for hay as they might have occasion for, and also gave them leave to take such materials out of the said forest to build their houses, and for other uses ; and such iron and lead as the monks found they might apply to their own use ; and if the monks or their servants found any flesh of wild beasts in the forest, *killed by Wolves*, they might take it to their own use.†

In 1348, we find that Alan, son and heir of Walter de Wulf hunte, paid a fine to the king of 2s. 4d. for his relief in respect of lands at Mansfield Woodhouse in the county of Nottingham, which he held by the service of hunting Wolves out of the forest of Shire-wood, if he should find any of them.‡

* Escheat, 15 & 16 Edw. III. No. 76, in Turr. Lond. See also Burton, "Monasticon Eboracense," p. 370. The Abbey of Fors, in Wensleydale, was founded in 1145 (Whitaker).

† Burton, loc. cit.

‡ De termino Trin. anno 21 Edw. III. Rot. 1. Harl. M.S. Brit. Mus. No. 34, p. 166. Blount, "Ancient Tenures," p. 258.

Thomas Engaine, dying without issue in 1368, was found to be seized of 14 yardlands and meadow, and 14s. 4d. rent, in Pightesle, in the county of Northampton, held by the service of finding, at his own proper costs, certain dogs for the destruction of Wolves, foxes, martens, cats, and other vermin within the counties of Northampton, Roteland, Oxford, Essex, and Buckingham.*

1377–1399. In Richard II.'s reign Wolves must have been common enough in the forests of Yorkshire, for in the account-rolls of Whitby Abbey, amongst the disbursements made between 1394 and 1396, we find the following entry of a payment for dressing Wolf skins :—

Pro tewyngt† xiiij pellium luporum . . . . 10. ixd.

Doubtless the skins of animals killed in some great raid made upon them at the instigation of the Abbey.

1399–1413. In Henry IV.'s reign, Sir Thomas de Aylesbury, knight, and Catharine his wife, held of the king, *in capite*, the manor of Laxton, *inter alia*, with appurtenances in the county of Northampton, by "grand serjeanty"—viz., by the service of taking Wolves, foxes, wild cats, and other vermin in the counties of Northampton, Rutland, Oxford, Essex, Huntingdon, and Buckingham.‡

Shakespeare has pictured wolves as existing in Kent

* Rot. fin. 42 Edw. III. m. 13. Dugdale's "Baronage," vol. i. p. 467; and Blount, "Ancient Tenures," p. 231.

† To "tew," or "taw," an obsolete word signifying to beat and dress leather with alum. Nares, "Glossary."

‡ Blount, op. cit. p. 260.

in the time of Henry VI. When the Duke of Suffolk lands at night upon the shore near Dover, he hears

> " Loud howling wolves arouse the jades
> That drag the tragic melancholy night."
> *Second Part of Henry VI*, act iv. sc. i.

This may or may not be a poetic license. At all events, no evidence on the subject is now forthcoming, and we must turn, therefore, to some more reliable source of information.

1422–1461. In the eleventh year of Henry VI. (1433), Sir Robert Plumpton, Knight, was seized of one bovate of land in Mansfield Woodhouse, in the county of Nottingham, called Wolf-hunt land, held by the service of winding a horn and chasing or frightening the Wolves in the forest of Shirewood.* This tenure is particularly referred to by the Rev. Samuel Pegge in his Paper "On the Horn as a Charter or Instrument of Conveyance."† A coloured plate of an ancient horn of the kind referred to, in the possession of the late Lord Ribblesdale, will be found in Whitaker's "History and Antiquities of the Deanery of Craven" (1805), p. 34.

In the seventeenth year of the reign of Henry VI., namely, in 1439, Robert Umfraville, a descendant, no doubt, of the Robert de Umfraville mentioned in 1076, held the castle of Herbotell and manor of Otterburn, of the king, *in capite*, by the service of keeping the valley and liberty of Riddesdale,

---

* Escaet. 11 Hen. VI. n. 5. Blount, p. 312.
† "Archæologia," vol. iii. p. 3. See also Thoroton, "Antiq. Nottingham," p. 273; and Strutt, "Sports and Pastimes," p. 19.

where the said castle and manor are situated, free from Wolves and robbers.*

1461–1483. If no particular mention of Wolves is to be met with in the days of Edward IV., his reign would nevertheless deserve notice here from the fact that at this period lived Juliana Barnes, or Berners, a lady of an ancient and illustrious house, who was commonly styled the Diana of her age, and who writ or compiled divers treatises on Hunting, Hawking, Fishing, and Heraldry.†

In her " Book of St. Albans," written about 1481, and first printed in 1486, she includes the Wolf amongst the beasts of venery, and thus instructs her readers on the subject :—

> " Wheresoeure ye fare by fryth or by fell :
> My dere chylde take hede how Tristran.‡ doo you tell,
> How many manere bestys of venery there were :
> Lysten to your dame, and she shall you lere.
> Foure maner bestys of venery there are :
> The fyrste of theym is the *harte*, the seconde is the *hare*,
> The *boore* is one of tho : the *wulfe* and not one mo."

The old books on hunting state that the season for hunting the Wolf was between the 25th of December and the 25th of March. This of course was only so long as Wolf-hunting was an amusement and a royal sport. As soon as it became a necessity, and a price was set on the animal's head, it was killed whenever and wherever it could be found.

1485–1509. Some time between these two dates,

* Madox, " Baronia Anglica," p. 244.

† Longstaffe, " Memoirs of the Life of Ambrose Barnes " (Surtees Society), 1867, p. 27.

‡ Manwood, in his " Forest Laws," mentions " Sir Tristram," an ancient forester, in his worthy treatise of hunting.

during the reign of Henry VII., it is probable that
the Wolf became finally extirpated in England,
although for nearly two centuries later, as will presently appear, it continued to hold out against its
persecutors in Scotland and Ireland. That it was
rare if not quite extinct in England about this time,
may be inferred from the circumstance that little or

A WOLF-HUNT. FROM AN ENGRAVING OF THE SIXTEENTH CENTURY.

no mention is made of it either in this or any
subsequent reign. It is true Professor Newton,
in his "Zoology of Ancient Europe," has stated
(p. 24) that the Wolf was found in the North
of England in the reign of Henry VIII., a statement
which has been also advanced, or copied, by other

writers,* but we have not met with any proof of this. Indeed, Professor Newton has lately been good enough to inform us that he has forgotten his authority for the statement, and thinks it possible a reference to the MS. of his essay, which was not preserved, would show that, by a typographical error, the numerals VIII. were printed for VII.

In Longstaffe's "Memoirs of the Life of Ambrose Barnes,"† it is stated that "his immediate ancestors held an estate of 500l. a year of the Earls of Rutland and Belvoir, one of whom (a Barnes of Hatford near Barnard Castle) was commonly called Ambrose 'Roast wolf,' from the many wolves which he hunted down and destroyed in the time of Henry VII."‡

In a footnote to this passage, the editor remarks that "the statement must be taken *cum grano salis*. Belvoir is not a title, and the Manners family did not become Earls of Rutland until 1525, in the reign of Henry VIII.§ On the other hand, the period of VII. is late for wolves, although Richmondshire might well yield some of the latest specimens in England. Doubtless they were familiarly associated with wildness of country long after their extinction. Many a tradition would linger in the families of their destroyers. Ambrose 'Roast Wolf' was probably a real person of some date or other."

* Wise's "New Forest, its History and its Scenery," p. 14.

† "Memoirs of the Life of Mr. Ambrose Barnes, late Merchant and sometime Alderman of Newcastle-upon-Tyne," p. 28. (Surtees Society, 1867.)

‡ See also Longstaffe's "Durham before the Conquest," p. 49.

§ It is possible that a typographical error may have been made here also, and that Ambrose "Roast Wolf" may have lived in the reign of Henry VIII., not Henry VII.

Within the precincts of Savernake Forest, the property of the Marquis of Ailesbury, near Marlborough, there is still existing a very old barn and part of a house, known as " Wolf Hall," or " Wulf-hall." It was the ancient residence of the Seymours, and when Henry VIII. married Lady Jane Seymour it was here that he came a-courting, here that he was married, and in this barn the wedding festivities are said to have taken place. In reply to an inquiry whether any tradition exists in the county to explain the name " Wolf Hall," the Rev. A. C. Smith, of Yatesbury Rectory, Calne, has obligingly written as follows :—" It is supposed to have had nothing to do with the animal ' Wolf,' but rather with ' Ulf,' the owner's name, if there was such a person, and in the Domesday record it is spelt ' Ulfhall.'* At the same time I must add that Leland in his Itinerary (ix. 36) calls it in Latin ' *Lupinum villa splendida*,' and again in his poem on the birth of the Prince of Wales, afterwards King Edward VI., *Incoluit villam, quæ nomine dicta lupinum.*† Bishop Turner also ("Bibl. Brit. Hibern.") speaks of certain epistles written by Edward, the future Protector, son of John Seymour, '*de Puteo Lupino, vulgo Wolf-hall.*' So I am not so certain that the derivation is not from the animal. At all events, it is quite clear that no place could be more fitted for Wolves than the wild extensive forest of Savernake hard by ; indeed, if Wolves existed at all in England now, that would be just the very harbour for them."

* See *Wilts Archæological Magazine*, June 1875, p. 143.
† " Genethliacon illustrissimi Eduardi Principis Cambriæ," 1543.

Many names of places compounded with "Wolf" still remain to attest probably the former existence of this animal in the neighbourhood. Wolmer—*i.e.*, Wolfmere or Wolvemere—is an instance of this. Wolferton is another. Besides these, we have Wolfscote, Derbyshire; Wolfhamcote, Warwickshire; Wolferlow, Hereford; Wolfs Castle, Pembroke; and Wolfpits, Radnorshire; the last named very suggestive, as indicating probably a former burial-place for the carcases of Wolves brought in during the period of their persecution in Wales. In the parish of West Chiltington, near Pulborough, Sussex, on the south edge of the lower greensand formation which overlooks the Weald, is a spot called " Wolfscrag," where, tradition says, the last Wolf of the Weald was killed. Three fields in the neighbourhood still bear the respective names of Great Den, Little Den, and Far Den fields.

Wolfenden in Rossendale, and Wolfstones in Cliviger (Lancashire), both attest the existence of this animal there when those names were imposed.* Many other instances, no doubt, might be adduced. In the parish of Beckermont, Cumberland, is a small hill, commonly called " Wotobank." A traditionary story, of great antiquity, says that a lord of Beckermont and his lady and servants were one time hunting the Wolf; during the chase this lord missed his lady; after a long and painful search, they at last,

* Whitaker, " History of Whalley," i. p. 74. " The first mention of Rossendale by name is in the memorable story of Liwlphus, Dean of Whalley, who, at a place called Ledmesgreve, cut off the tail of a Wolf in hunting " (tom. cit. p. 316.)

to his inexpressible sorrow, found her body lying on this hill or bank, slain by a Wolf, and the ravenous beast in the very act of tearing it to pieces, till frightened by the dogs. In the first transports of his grief the first words that he uttered were, " Woe to this bank !" since which time it has been commonly called " Wotobank."*

In Lancashire, Dr. Whitaker particularly mentions the great forests of Blackburnshire and Bowland as " among the last retreats of the Wolf."†

The " wolds" of Yorkshire appear, from the dates of parish books, to have been infested with Wolves perhaps later than any other part of England.

" In the entries at Flixton, Hackston, and Folkston, in the East Riding of Yorkshire," says Blaine, " are still to be seen memoranda of payments made for the destruction of Wolves at a certain rate per head. They used to breed in the 'cars' below, amongst the rushes, furze, and bogs, and in the night-time to come up from their dens ; and, unless the sheep had been previously driven into the town, or the shepherds were indefatigably vigilant, great numbers were sure to be destroyed."‡

Apparently, however, some error has been made in the orthography of the localities referred to. Flixton is in the parish of Folkton, near Scarboro'. We can-

* Hutchinson, " Hist. and Antiq. Cumberland" (1794), vol. ii. p. 16. Upon this tradition was founded an " elegant elegiac tale" by Mrs. Cowley, which will be found prefixed to the second volume of the work quoted.

† Op. cit. i. p. 205. The last herd of red deer was destroyed there in 1805.

‡ Blaine's " Encyclop. Rural Sports " (1858), p. 105.

41

not find that there is any such place as "Hackston;" but Staxton adjoins the other places named, and is in the parish of Willerby. The Vicar of Willerby, the Rev. G. Day, at our request most obligingly instituted a search, but could not succeed in finding any parish books of any kind to throw light on the subject. He writes : "There are no gentry resident in this parish, and the churchwardens have been tenant-farmers for generations. Of course great changes have occurred within the last, say, fifty years, amongst these tenant-farmers. Many names have altogether disappeared from the parish roll, and it is thought probable by some of the old farmers here that church-wardens in past days having left their farms and gone to other parishes took the parish books with them, and that these have either been destroyed or are lying hid in some descendant's lumber-room."

In a Paper "On Druidical Remains in the Parish of Halifax, Yorkshire," by the Rev. John Watson, M.A., F.S.A.,* the author says that "in the township of Barkisland is a small ring of stones, now called (1771) by the name of the *wolf-fold*. It is but a few yards in diameter, but the exact measurement of it I have lost or mislaid.

"The stones of which it consists are not erect, but lie in a confused heap like the ruins of a building. This place I took at first, from its name, to have been either a decoy for the taking of wolves, or a place to secure them in for the purpose of hunting ; but observing that Mr. Borlase (p. 198) has attributed

* "Archæologia," vol. ii. p 355.

some such little cirques to the Druids, I have mentioned it here for the further examination of anti-
quaries, who are desired to take notice that if ever
there was a wall here of any strength, the best stones
must have been carried away ; for what are left are
extremely rude, and totally unfit of themselves to
compose any sort of building; also that these few
insignificant pebbles, as they now appear, must be of
considerable antiquity, as well as once have been of
considerable account, because they give the name of
Ringstone Edge to a large tract of land around them."

The late Wm. Hamper, F.S.A., in some learned
observations on certain ancient pillars of memorial
called Hoar Stones ("Archæologia," xxv.), gives a list
of such as were known to him, and, in particular,
mentions (p. 53) the *wolf-stone*, a single merestone,
one immense natural block on Dr. Whitaker's estate,
which, in all probability, was erected to commemorate
some notable slaughter of Wolves in days gone by.

The fur of the Wolf was formerly used for trimming
robes, and was employed for this purpose at least as
late as the time of Elizabeth. In a will dated 1573
preserved in the Registry of the Prerogative Court
of Canterbury the following clause occurs :—

" Also I give unto my son Tyble my sherte gown
faced with Wolf and laid with Billement's lace ; also I
give unto my brother Cowper my other sherte gown
faced with foxe ; also I give unto Thomas Walker
my night gown faced with coney, with one lace also,
and my ready [ruddy] colored hose."

Where the testator procured the Wolf-skin it is of

course impossible to say, but it is noticeable that no foreign furs (such as sable, ermine, and lynx) are mentioned in his Will; the only furs disposed of besides Wolf being those of indigenous animals—the fox and the coney.

HISTORICAL EVIDENCE.—SCOTLAND.

In a preceding page it was incidentally remarked that the Wolf survived in Scotland to a much later date than was the case in England. The reason is pretty obvious. Long after the animal had been extirpated in England the condition of the country in North Britain remained eminently suited to its nature. Vast tracts of forest and moor, rugged and well-nigh impenetrable in parts, entire districts of unreclaimed and uncultivated land, the absence of roads, and the consequent difficulty of communication between scattered and thinly populated hamlets, long contributed to shelter the Wolf not only from final extinction but from the incessant persecution which had driven it from the south.

The aspect of the country in Scotland at the date to which we refer may be imagined from a remark of John Taylor, the Water Poet, who in 1618 travelled on foot from London to Edinburgh. When visiting Braemar, he says, " I was the space of twelve days before I saw either house, cornfield, or habitation of any creature, but deer, wild horses, Wolves, and such like creatures, which made me doubt that I should never have seen a house again."

It must not be supposed, however, that the Wolf

at any time lived unmolested in Scotland. As the herdsman's foe, it was always regarded as a beast to be pursued and killed whenever and wherever practicable, and from the earliest times the chase of the Wolf was considered by kings and nobles to be one of the most exciting and enjoyable of field-sports.

We learn from Holinshed that Dorvadil, the fourth King of the Scots, " set all his pleasure on hunting and keeping of houndes and greyhoundes, ordayning that every householder should find him two houndes and one greyhounde. If a hunter chanced in following the game to lose an eye or a limme, so that he were not able to helpe himselfe after that time, he made a statute that he should be founde of the common treasury. He that killed a Wolf should have an oxe for his paines. This beast, indeed, the Scottish men even from the beginning used to pursue in al they might devise, because the same is suche an enemie to cattayle, wherein consisted the chiefest portion of all their wealth and substance."*

Of a later king, Ederus, we are told that his "chiefe delighte was altogyther in hunting and keeping of houndes and greyhoundes, to chase and pursue wild beastes, and namely the Woolfe the herdsman's foe, by means whereof his advancement was muche the more acceptable amongst the nobles, who in those dayes were whollye given to that kynde of pleasure and pastyme."†

* Holinshed's " Chronicles of Scotland," 1577, p. 13.
† Holinshed, tom. cit. p. 27

Ferquhard II., who died A.D. 668, is said to have proved so bad a king that Colman, Bishop of Lindisfarne, declared the vengeance of God would overtake him. " And sure his wordes proved true ; for within a moneth after, as the same Ferquhard followed in chase of a Wolfe, the beast being enraged by pursuite of the houndes, flew back uppon the king, and snatching at him, did wounde and byte him righte sore in one of his sides, immediately whereupon, whether through anguishe of his hurt, or by some other occasion, he fell into a most filthie disease."*

The sport enjoyed in Scotland in former days must have been incomparable. Bellenden, the translator of Hector Boece, says, that in the forests of Caledonia there were "gret plente of haris, hartis, hindis, dayis, rais, *Wolffis*, wild hors, and toadis," (foxes), and he particularly mentions " the *Wolffis* " as being "rycht noysum to the tame bestiall in all partis of Scotland."

In the reign of Malcolm IV. (1153–1165) Robert de Avenel granted to the monks of Melrose the right of pasturage in his lands in Eskdale, reserving to himself the privileges of the feudal baron, to pursue the wild boar, the deer, and the stag. One of his successors questioned several of the claims to which the grantees considered themselves entitled, and it was ultimately decided in 1235, in presence of King Alexander II., that they had no right to hunt over the lands in question, and were restricted from setting

* Holinshed, p. 148.

traps, *excepting for Wolves.** It seems that, in order to protect their flocks, the monks of Melrose were in the habit of setting traps for Wolves as early as the reign of William the Lion (1165-1214).† Wolfclyde, a part of the barony of Culter, in Lanarkshire, passed by grant to the Abbey of Melrose in 1431.‡

In a grant of Alexander II. (1214-1249) to the monks of Melrose, in Ettrick Forest, mention is made of "Wulfhope," a name still familiar in the south of Roxburghshire.§

In 1283, there was an allowance made for "one hunter of Wolves" at Stirling.‖

In 1427, in the reign of James I. of Scotland, an Act was passed for the destruction of wolves in that kingdom. Further Acts with the like object were passed in 1457, in 1525, and in 1577. The Act of 1525, however, is merely a modernized version of the law of 1427, which is referred to in the statute of 1577 as "the auld act made tharon."

The law required "that ilk baron within his barony in gangand time of the year sall chase and seek the qulelpes of Wolves and gar slay them. And the baron sall give to the man that slays the Woolfe in his barony and brings the baron the head, twa shillings. And when the baron ordains to hunt and chase the Woolfe, the tenants sall rise with the baron. And that the barons hunt in their baronies and chase the

---

* Morton's "Monastic Annals of Teviotdale," pp. 273, 274.
† Chalmers' "Caledonia," ii. p. 132.   Chart. Mel. 91.
‡ Morton, op. cit. p. 276.
§ Chalmers' "Caledonia," ii. p. 132.
‖ Innes' "Scotland in the Middle Ages," p. 125.

Woolfes four times a year, and als oft as onie Woolfe
beis seen within the barony. And that na man seek
the Woolfe with schott, but allanerly in the time of
hunting them." The duty of summoning the people
for a Wolf-hunt devolved upon the "schireffs" or
"bailyis," three times a year, between St. Mark's Day
(April 25th) and Lammas (August 1st), for, as the
Act states, "that is the tyme of their quhelpes."
The penalty for disregarding this summons was "ane
wedder," "quhatever he be that rysse not." On
the other hand, it was enacted that whoever slew a
Wolf "sall haif of ilk householder of that parochin
that the Woolfe is slayne within, a penny."

The Act of James II.'s time (1457), provided
that "they that slayis ane Woolfe sall bring the
head to the schireffe, baillie, or baronne, and he sall
be debtour to the slayer for the summe foresaide.
And quhatsumever hee bee that slayis ane Woolfe,
and bringis the head to the schireffe, lord, baillie, or
baronne, he sall have sex pennyes."*

In some active instances, the exertion of these
statutes might have cleared local districts, and a
remarkable example of success was given by a woman
—Lady Margaret Lyon, Baroness to Hugh third
Lord Lovat. This lady having been brought up in
the low country, at a distance from the Wolves, was
probably the more affected by their neighbourhood,
and caused them to be so vigorously pursued in the

* "Laws of the Parliament of Scotland," folio, 1781, pp. 18, 19.
See also Glendook's Scots Acts, 7 James I. c. 104, and 14 James II.
c. 88.

Aird, that they were exterminated out of their principal hold in that range. According to the Wardlaw MS., "she was a stout bold woman, a great huntress; she would have travelled in our hills a-foot, and perhaps outwearied good footmen. She purged Mount Caplach of the Wolves." Mount Caplach is the highest range of the Aird running parallel to the Beauly Frith, behind Moniach and Lentron. Though the place of the lady's seat is now forgotten, its existence is still remembered, and said to have been at a pass where she sat when the woods were driven for the Wolves, not only to see them killed, but to shoot at them with her own arrows. The period of her repression of the Wolves is indicated by the succession of her husband to the lordship of Lovat, which was in 1450, and it is therefore probable that the "purging" of Mount Caplach was begun soon after that date.*

Such partial expulsions, however, had little effect upon the general "herd" of Wolves, which, fostered by the great Highland forests, increased at intervals to an alarming extent. During the reign of James IV. (1488–1513), rewards continued to be paid for the slaughter of Wolves in Scotland, and we learn the value of a Wolf's head in those days from the accounts of the Lord High Treasurer.† For in-

* MS. History of the Frasers, in the library of Lord Lovat (p. 44). Also the curious account of the North Highlands called the Wardlaw MS. in the possession of Mr. Thompson, Inverness (p. 67).

† Extracts from these accounts will be found in Pitcairn's "Criminal Trials in Scotland," vol. i. p. 116.

stance, under date "October 24th, 1491," we find this entry :—

"Item, til a fallow brocht ye king ij wolfis in Lythgow . . . Vs."

In the time of James V. their numbers and ravages were formidable. At that period great part of Ross, Inverness, almost the whole of Cromarty, and large tracts of Perth and Argyleshire, were covered with forests of pine, birch, and oak, the remains of which continued to our time in Braemar, Invercauld, Rothiemurchus, Arisaig, the banks of Loch Ness, Glen Strath-Farar, and Glen Garrie; and it is known from history and tradition that the braes of Moray, Nairn, and Glen Urcha, the glens of Lochaber, and Loch Erroch, the moors of Rannach, and the hills of Ardgour were covered in the same manner.* All these clouds of forests were more or less frequented by Wolves. Boethius mentions their numbers and devastation in his time;† and in various districts where they last remained, the traditions of their haunts are still familiarly remembered. Loch Sloigh and Strath Earn are still celebrated for their resort, and in 1848 there were living in Lochaber old people who related from their predecessors, that, when all the country from the Lochie to Loch Erroch was covered by a continuous pine forest, the eastern tracts upon the Blackwater and the wild wilderness stretching towards Rannach were so dense and

* MacFarlane's Geographical Collections. MS. Bibl. Facult. Jurid. ii. 192. Quoted in Stuart's " Lays of the Deer Forest."
† " Scot. Hist." fol. 7.

infested by the rabid droves, that they were almost impassable.*

In 1528 the Earl of Athole entertained the king, James V., with a great hunt which lasted three days. "It is said, at this tyme, in Atholl and Stratherdaill boundis, thair was slaine threttie scoir of hart and hynd, with other small beasties, sich as roe and roebuck, *Woulff*, fox, and wild cattis."†

A story is told of one John Eldar, a clergyman of Caithness, who on the death of James V. journeyed to England to present to Henry VIII. a project for the union of the two kingdoms. Being asked to explain the meaning of the name "redshanks," at that time given to the Highlanders, he said, "They call us in Scotland, 'redshanks,' please it your Majesty to understand, that we of all people can tolerate, suffer, and away best with cold : for both summer and winter (except when the frost is most vehement) going always bare-legged and bare-footed, our delight and pleasure is in hunting of red deer, *Wolves*, foxes, and graies [badgers] whereof we abound and have great plenty. Therefore, in so much as we use and delight so to go always, the tender, delicate gentlemen of Scotland call us 'redshanks.'"‡

Harrison, who wrote in Elizabeth's time, says that though the English "may safelie boast of their securitie in respect to wild animals, yet cannot the Scots do the like in everie point within their king-

---

* Stuart's "Lays of the Deer Forest," vol. ii. pp. 231, 232.
† Robert Lindsay, "Chronicles of Scotland," ii. p. 346.
‡ Pinkerton's "History of Scotland," ii. p. 396.

dome, sith they have greevous *Woolfes* and cruell foxes, beside some other of like disposition continuallie conversant among them, to the general hindrance of their husbandmen and no small damage unto the inhabiters of those quarters."*

William Barclay, who was a native of Aberdeenshire, and spent the early part of his life at the Court of Queen Mary, accompanied her Majesty on an excursion to the Highlands, and has left a curious account† of a royal hunt at which he was present, and which was organized for the Queen by John, fourth Earl of Athole, in 1563. Two thousand Highlanders were employed to drive all the deer from the woods and hills of Athole, Badenach, Mar, Moray, and the surrounding country. After mentioning incidentally that the Queen ordered one of the fiercest dogs to be slipped at a Wolf—" *Laxatus enim reginæ jussu, atque immissus in lupum, insignis admodum ac ferox canis* "—Barclay concludes his account of the "drive" with the statement that there were killed that very day 360 deer, 5 Wolves, and some roes.

According to Holinshed, Wolves were very destructive to the flocks in Scotland during the reign of James VI. in 1577. At this time they were so numerous throughout the greater part of the Highlands, that in the winter it was necessary to provide houses, or "spittals" as they were termed, to afford

* Harrison's "Description of England," prefixed to Holinshed's "Chronicles," i. p. 378.
† "De Regno et regali Potestate," &c., 4to, 1600, p. 279.

52

lodgings to travellers who might be overtaken by night where there was no place of shelter. Hence the origin of the Spittal of Glen Shae, and similar appellations in other places.

Camden, whose "Britannia" was published in 1586, asserts that Wolves at that date were common in many parts of Scotland, and particularly refers to Strathnavern.

" The county," he says, " hath little cause to brag of its fertility. By reason of the sharpness of the air it is very thinly inhabited, and thereupon extremely infested with the fiercest of Wolves, which, to the great damage of the county, not only furiously set upon cattle, but even upon the owners themselves, to the manifest danger of their lives. In so much that not only in this, but in many other parts of Scotland, the sheriffs and respective inhabitants are bound by Act of Parliament, in their several sheriffdoms, to go a hunting thrice every year to destroy the Wolves and their whelps."[*]

Bishop Lesley, writing towards the close of the sixteenth century, complains much of the prevalence of Wolves at that period, and of their ferocity.[†]

" About this time there was nothing but the petty flock of sheep, or herd of a few milk-cows, grazed round the farm-house, and folded nightly for fear of the Wolf, or more cunning depredators."[‡]

[*] Camden, " Britannia," vol. ii. p. 1279. Bishop Gibson, in his edition, has a marginal note to this passage—" No Wolves now in Scot:aud " (1772).
[†] " De Origine, Moribus et Rebus Scotorum."
[‡] Irvine's " Scotch Legal Antiquities," p. 264.

Towards the end of the sixteenth and beginning of the seventeenth centuries large tracts of forests in the Highlands were purposely cut down or burned, as the only means of expelling the Wolves which there abounded.

> "These hills and glens and wooded wilds can tell
> How many wolves and boars and deer then fell."
> Campbell's Grampians Desolate, p. 102.

" On the south side of Beann Nevis, a large pine forest, which extended from the western bräes of Lochaber to the Black Water and the mosses of Rannach, was burned to expel the Wolves. In the neighbourhood of Loch Sloi, a tract of woods nearly twenty miles in extent was consumed for the same purpose."*

John Taylor, the Water Poet, who made his " Pennyles Pilgrimage " into Scotland in 1618, saw Wolves in Braemar. He writes : " My good Lord of Mar having put me into shape, I rode with him from his house, where I saw the ruins of an old castle, called the castle of Kindroghit. It was built by King Malcolm Canmore (for a hunting-house), who reigned in Scotland when Edward the Confessor, Harold, and Norman William reigned in England. I speak of it because it was the last house that I saw in those parts ; for I was the space of twelve days after before I saw either house, cornfield, or habitation of any creature, but deer, wild horses, *Wolves*,

---

* Notes to Sobieski Stuart's "Last Deer of Beann Doran." See his " Poems" published in 1822 under the assumed name of James Hay Allan.

and such-like creatures, which made me doubt that I should never have seen a house again."*

Years later, as we learn from Sir Robert Gordon, the Wolf was still included amongst the wild animals of Sutherlandshire. He says the forests and "schases" in that county were "verie profitable for feiding of bestiall, and delectable for hunting, being full of reid deer and roes, *Woulffs*, foxes, wyld catts, brocks, skuyrells, whittrets, weasels, otters, martrixes, hares, and fumarts."†

In 1621 the price paid in Sutherlandshire for the killing of one Wolf according to statute was 6*l.* 13*s.* 4*d.*

Wolf-skins are mentioned in 1661 in a Customs Roll of Charles II.,‡ whence it appears that two ounces of silver were paid " for ilk two daker."§

Twenty years later, if we are to credit the statement of Sir Robert Sibbald, whose "Scotia Illustrata" was published in 1684, the animal had become extinct. His words are: *Lupi olim frequentes erant, quidam etiam de Caledoniis ursis loquuntur.*

* " The Pennyles Pilgrimage, or the Moneylesse Perambulation of John Taylor, alias the King's Majesties Water Poet. How he travailed on foot from London to Edenborough in Scotland. With his description of his entertainment in all places of his journey and a true report of the unmatchable hunting in the Brea of Marre and Badenoch in Scotland." 4to, London, 1681.

† " Genealogical History of the Earldom of Sutherland, from its origin to the year 1630."

‡ See Glendook's " Scots Acts," Charles II., p. 36.

§ The word "daker" or "dicker" (Greek δεκα, *ten*) is still in use in the leather trade, and means a roll of ten skins. It was anciently spelt "dyker" or "dykker," and the market-toll was a penny each "dyker." See the Durham Household Book, 1530–1534, pp. 107, 205, where this word frequently occurs.

Sed horum genus deletum et ex insulâ exterminatum est."*

Pennant states that the Wolf became extinct in Scotland in 1680, when the last of the race was slain by Sir Ewen Cameron of Lochiel.† He adds that he had travelled " into almost every corner of that country, but could not learn that there remained even the memory of these animals among the oldest people."‡

From more recent investigation, however, it is clear that Sir Robert Sibbald and Pennant were both mistaken, for not only were Wolves slain in Scotland subsequently to 1680, but numerous traditions concerning these animals survived in the country to at least as recent a date as 1848.

Traditions.—In a Gaelic forest lay " of a remote period, the date and author of which are uncertain," the Wolf is thus referred to as inhabiting the ancient pine woods of Scotland :—

> " Chì mì Sgòrr-eild' air bruaich a' ghlinn'
> An goir a' chuthag gu-bìnn an dòs.
> 'Us gòrm mheall-àild' nam mìle guibhas
> Nan *lùb*, nan earba, 's nan lon."

> " I see the ridge of hinds, the steep of the sloping glen
> The wood of cuckoos at its foot,
> The blue height of a thousand pines,
> Of *wolves*, and roes, and elks.§

* " Scotia Illustrata, sive Prodromus Historiæ Naturalis," folio, 1684, pars ii. p. 9.

† Surtees gives the date of the death of the last Wolf in Scotland as 1682. "History and Antiquities of the County of Durham,"vol. ii. p. 172.

‡ " British Zoology," vol. i. p. 88 ; and " Tour in Scotland," vol. i. p. 206.

§ From ' The Aged Bard's Wish,' given in Stuart's " Lays of the Deer Forest," ii. p. 9.

Other Gaelic names for the Wolf are *madadh alluidh*, commonly used ; *faol chu*, and *alla mhadadh*, all of which are composed of an epithet and a word which now means dog.* It is also called *faol* and *mac tire*, " earth's son."†

In Scrope's " Days of Deer-Stalking" (p. 109) is related an adventure with a Wolf that happened to Macpherson of Braekaely, when he had charge of the forest of Benalder, and was furnished to the author by Cluny Macpherson, chief of Clanchattan.

" He sallied forth one morning, as he was wont, in quest of venison, accompanied by his servant. In the course of their travel, they found a Wolf den—a Wolf being at that time by no means a rarity in the forest. Macpherson asked his servant whether he would prefer going into the den to destroy the cubs, or remaining outside to guard against the approach of the old ones. The servant, preferring what appeared to be an uncertain to a certain danger, said he would remain without ; but here Sandy had miscalculated, for, to his great dismay, the dam came raging to the mouth of the cave, which no sooner did he see than he took to his heels incontinently, without even warning his master of the danger. Macpherson, however, being an active, resolute man, and expert at his weapons, succeeded in killing the old Wolf as well as the cubs."

This Macpherson of Braekaely was commonly

---

* Pinkerton's " Enquiry into the Early History of Scotland," vol. ii. p. 85.

† Campbell's " Tales of the West Highlands," vol. i. p. 274.

called Callum Beg, or little Malcolm ; and there is reason to believe that he was one of those who fought in the famous battle of the Inch of Perth in the reign of Robert III. (1390–1406.)

In the districts where Wolves last abounded, says Stuart in the "Lays of the Deer Forest," many traditions of their history and haunts have descended to our time. The greatest number preserved in one circle were in the neighbourhood of Strath Earn.

At Inver-Rua, on the Spean, and consequently within the lands of Keppach, there lived a Campbell of the Slioched Chailein Mhic-Dhonnacha, or Glen Urcha race. Although thus a tenant of one of the principal branches of the Clan Donald, and removed to the distance of forty miles from his *cean tighe*, he continued to pay his " calps " to his blood chief, the Knight of Loch Awe. This tax was a heifer, which was paid annually, and it happened one year that a short time before it fell due, the beast was killed on her pasture and half eaten by a Wolf. Campbell left what remained to tempt his return, and on the following night, watching the carcase, he shot the Wolf from behind a stone. Not being able, however, to afford another " calp," he flayed the dead heifer, and sent the torn hide to MacChailein Mhic-Donnacha, with a message that it was all which he had to show for his "calp;" upon which the chief observed, that he had sent sufficient parchment to write his discharge.

This is said to have happened in the time of Sir Duncan Campbell, called " *Donacha dubh a' Cur-*

58

rach'd," " Black Duncan of the Hood," so called from
having been the last person of his rank who bore the
old Highland hood in Argyllshire, and who lived in
the reign of James VI. (1567–1603).

Several traditions relative to Wolves are evidences
of the accuracy with which oral relations have been
transmitted through many generations, which is
exemplified by the familiarity and fidelity with which
they retain allusions to objects and customs disused
for two hundred years.

An example of this occurs in an account of the
slaughter of a remarkable Wolf killed by one of the
lairds of Chisholm in Gleann Chon-fhiadh, or the
Wolves' Glen, a noted retreat of these animals in
the sixteenth century.

The animal in question had made her den in a
" càrn," or pile of loose rocks, whence she made
excursions in every direction until she became the
terror of the country. At length the season of her
cubs increasing her ferocity, and having killed some
of the neighbouring people, she attracted the enter-
prise of the Laird of Chisholm and his brother, then
two gallant young hunters, and they resolved to
attempt her destruction. For this they set off
alone from Strath Glass, and having tracked her
to her den, discovered by her traces that she was
abroad ; but detecting the little pattering feet of the
cubs in the sand about the mouth of the den, the
elder crept into the chasm with his drawn dirk, and
began the work of vengeance on the litter. While
he was thus occupied, the Wolf returned, and infu-

riated by the expiring yelps of her cubs, rushed at the entrance, regardless of the younger Chisholm, who made a stroke at her with his spear, but such was her velocity, that he missed her as she darted past, and broke the point of his weapon. His brother, however, met the animal as she entered, and being armed with the left-handed *lámhainn chruaidh*, or steel gauntlet, much used by the Highlanders and Irish, as the Wolf rushed open-mouthed upon him, he thrust the iron fist into her jaws, and stabbed her in the breast with his dirk, while his brother, striking at her flank with the broken spear, after a desperate struggle she was drawn out dead.

The spear and the left-handed gauntlet referred to in this tradition are arms mentioned by Spencer, Leslie, and other authorities, as characteristic of the Highlanders and Irish in the days of Queen Mary.*

It is true they retained the use of such weapons as late as their muster called the "Highland Host" in 1678.† But no such remains appeared at Cillie-chranchie, and it is therefore probable that the story has descended from the time of Charles II.

Another story is on record of a Wolf killed by a woman of Cre-lebhan, near Strui, on the north side of Strath Glass. She had gone to Strui a little before Christmas to borrow a girdle (a thick circular plate of iron, with an iron loop handle at one side for lifting, and used for baking bread). Having procured it,

* See Spencer's "Views of Ireland;" Derrick's "Image of Ireland;" Leslie, "De Origine, Moribus et Rebus Scotorum;" and a print in the Douce Collection, Bodl. Lib. G. vi. 47.

† Wodrow MS. Bibl. Facult. Jurid., xcix. No. 29.

and being on her way home, she sat down upon an old càrn to rest and gossip With a neighbour, when suddenly a scraping of stones and rustling of dead leaves were heard, and the head of a Wolf protruded from a crevice at her side. Instead of fleeing in alarm, however, "she dealt him such a blow on the skull with the full swing of her iron discus, that it brained him on the stone which served for his emerging head."

This tradition was probably one of the latest in the district, and seems to have belonged to a period when the Wolves were near their end. Their last great outbreak in the time of Queen Mary led to more vigorous measures, which in the time of Charles II. reduced their ranks to so small a number that in some districts their extinction is believed to have followed soon after that period. Thus, in Lochaber, the last *in that part of the country* is said to have been killed by Sir Ewen Cameron in 1680, which Pennant misunderstood to have been the last of the species in Scotland.*

Some traditionary notices there are of the destruction of the last Wolves seen in Sutherlandshire, consisting of four old ones and some whelps which were killed about the same time at three different places,—at Auchumore in Assynt, in Halladale, and in Glen Loth—widely distant from each other, and as late as between the years 1690 and 1700.

The death of the last Wolf and her cubs on the

* In the Sale Catalogue of the "London Museum" which was disposed of by auction in April, 1818, there is the following entry: "Lot 832. Wolf—a noble animal in a large glass case. The last Wolf killed in Scotland by Sir E. Cameron."

eastern coast of Sutherlandshire, says Scrope, was attended with remarkable circumstances.

"A man named Polson, of Wester Helmsdale, accompanied by two lads, one of them his son and the other an active herdboy, tracked a Wolf to a rocky mountain gully which forms the channel of the Burn of Sledale in Glen Loth. Here he discovered a narrow fissure in the midst of large fragments of rock, which led apparently to a larger opening or cavern below, which the Wolf might use as his den. The two lads contrived to squeeze themselves through the fissure to examine the interior, whilst Polson kept guard on the outside.

" The boys descended through the narrow passage into a small cavern, which was evidently a Wolf's den, for the ground was covered with bones and horns of animals, feathers, and eggshells, and the dark space was somewhat enlivened by five or six active Wolf cubs. Polson desired them to destroy these; and soon after he heard their feeble howling. Almost at the same time, to his great horror, he saw approaching him a full-grown Wolf, evidently the dam, raging furiously at the cries of her young. As she attempted to leap down, at one bound Polson instinctively threw himself forward and succeeded in catching a firm hold of the animal's long and bushy tail, just as the fore-part of her body was within the narrow entrance of the cavern. He had unluckily placed his gun against a rock when aiding the boys in their descent, and could not now reach it. Without apprising the lads below of their imminent peril, the stout hunter kept a firm grip of the Wolf's tail, which he wound round his left arm, and although the maddened brute scrambled and twisted and strove with all her might to force herself down to the rescue of her cubs, Polson was just able with the exertion of all his strength to keep her from going forward. In the midst of this singular struggle, which passed in silence, his son within the cave, finding the light excluded from above, asked in Gaelic, 'Father, what is keeping the light from us?' 'If the root of the tail breaks,' replied he, 'you will soon know that.' Before long, however, the man contrived to get hold of his hunting-knife, and stabbed the Wolf in the most vital parts he could reach. The enraged animal now attempted to turn and face her foe, but the hole was too narrow to allow of this; and when Polson saw his danger he squeezed her forward, keeping her jammed in whilst he repeated his stabs as rapidly as he could, until the animal being mortally wounded, was easily dragged back and finished.

"These were the last Wolves killed in Sutherland, and the den was between Craig-Rhadich and Craig-Voakie, by the narrow Glen of Loth, a place replete with objects connected with traditionary legends."*

This story was related by the Duke of Sutherland's head forester in 1848 to Mr. J. F. Campbell, who has narrated it in his "Popular Tales of the West Highlands," vol. i. p. 273.

"Every district," says Stuart in his "Lays of the Deer Forest," "has its 'last' Wolf," and there were

---

* Scrope's "Days of Deer Stalking," p. 374.

probably several which were later than that killed by Sir Ewen Cameron.* The "last" of Strath Glass was killed at Gusachan according to tradition "at no very distant period." The "last" in Glen Urchard on the east side of the valley between Loch Leiter and Shengly, at a place called ever since *Slochd à mhadaidh*—*i.e.*, the Wolf's den ; and the last of the Findhorn and also (as there seems every reason to believe) the last of the species in Scotland, at a place between Fi-Giuthas and Pall-à-chrocain, and according to popular chronology no longer ago than the year 1743. The district in which he was killed was well calculated to have given harbour to the last of a savage race. All the country round his haunt was an extent of wild and desolate moorland hills, beyond which, in the west, there was retreat to the vast wilderness of the Monaidh-laith, an immense tract of desert mountains utterly uninhabited, and unfrequented except by summer herds and herdsmen, but, when the cattle had retired, abundantly re-plenished with deer and other game, to give ample provision to the "wild dogs." The last of their race was killed by MacQueen of Pall-à-chrocain, who died in the year 1797, and was the most celebrated "carnach" of the Findhorn for an unknown period. Of gigantic stature, six feet seven inches in height, he was equally remarkable for his strength, courage, and celebrity as a deer-stalker, and had the best

* A portrait of this devoted partizan of the house of Stuart was exhibited at the meeting of the British Association at Aberdeen in 1859.

"long dogs" or deer-hounds in the country. One winter's day, about the year before mentioned, he received a message from the Laird of MacIntosh that a large "black beast," supposed to be a Wolf, had appeared in the glens, and the day before killed two children, who with their mother were crossing the hills from Calder, in consequence of which a "Tainchel" or "gathering" to drive the country was called to meet at a tryst above Fi-Giuthas, where MacQueen was invited to attend with his dogs. He informed himself of the place where the children had been killed, the last tracks of the Wolf, and the conjectures of his haunt, and promised his assistance.

In the morning the "Tainchel" had long assembled, and MacIntosh waited with impatience, but MacQueen did not arrive. His dogs and himself were, however, auxiliaries too important to be left behind, and they continued to wait until the best of a hunter's morning was gone, when at last he appeared, and MacIntosh received him with an irritable expression of disappointment.

" *Ciod e a chabhag?*" ("What was the hurry?") said he of Pall-à-chrocain.

MacIntosh gave an indignant retort, and all present made some impatient reply.

MacQueen lifted his plaid and drew the black, bloody head of the Wolf from under his arm!

" *Sin e dhùibh !*" ("There it is for you !") said he, and tossed it on the grass in the midst of the surprised circle.

MacIntosh expressed great joy and admiration,

and gave him the land called Sean-achan for meal to his dogs."

Sir Thomas Dick Lauder, in his "Account of the Moray Floods of August, 1829," tells the story of the Wolf killed in that district by MacQueen of Pall-à-chrocain, but lays the scene of the exploit in the parish of Moy, in the county of Inverness, which, although within the bounds of the ancient province of Moray, is far beyond the present limits of the forest of Tarnaway.

Sir Thomas gives the very words which MacQueen is said to have used in describing to the chief of MacIntosh how he killed the wolf: "As I came through the *slochk (i.e.,* ravine) by east the hill there," said he, as if talking of some everyday occurrence, "I foregathered wi' the beast. My long dog there turned him. I buckled wi' him, and dirkit him, and syne whuttled his craig (*i.e.,* cut his throat), and brought awa' his countenance for fear he might come alive again, for they are very precarious creatures." In reward for his bravery, his chief is said to have bestowed on him a gift of the lands of Sean-achan "to yield meal for his good greyhounds in all time coming." Sir Thomas Lauder has preserved another tradition of the extirpation of the Wolf in Morayshire, when two old Wolves and their cubs were killed by one man in a ravine under the Knock of Braemory, near the source of the Burn of Newton.

In the old "Statistical Account of Scotland," edited by Sir John Sinclair, and published in twenty-one volumes between the years 1791 and

1799, a few entries relating to the Wolf occur, but they are neither numerous nor important. Mr J. A. Harvie Brown, who has lately examined the entire series of volumes for another purpose, has obligingly communicated the following particulars: " The woods in Blair Athole and Strowan in Perthshire once afforded shelter for Wolves (vol. ii. p. 486), as did also the district around Cathcart in Renfrewshire (vol. v. p. 347). In Orkney it appears they were unknown (vol. vii. p. 546). The wilds and mountains of Glenorchay and Innishail in Argyllshire are noted as being formerly haunted by these animals, whence they issued to attack not only the flock but their owners (vol. viii. p. 343). Towards the west end of the parish of Birse in Aberdeenshire there is a place in the Grampians still known (1793) by the name of the Wolf-holm (vol. ix. p. 108). Ubster, a town in Caithness (from 'Wolfster,' Danish or Icelandic), appears to have received its name either from its being of old a place infested with Wolves, or from a person of the name of Wolf (vol. x. p. 32). In Banffshire the last Wolf is said to have been killed in the parish of Kirkmichael about 1644" (vol. xii. p. 447).

Dr. Robert Brown heard a tradition in Caithnessshire that the wood on the hills of Yarrow, near Wick, was cut down about the year 1500 by the enraged dwellers in the district on account of its harbouring Wolves, and that the last Wolf in that neighbourhood was killed between Brabster and Freswick in a hollow called Wolfsburn.

The place where the last Wolf that infested Monteith was killed is a romantic cottage south-west of the mill of Milling, in the parish and barony of Port.*

"The devastations of Oliver Cromwell in the vast oak and fir woods of Lochaber are well known, and in 1848 the old people still retained traditions of the native clearances in the same century, when the great tracts south of Loch Treig and upon the Blackwater were set on fire to exterminate the Wolves."†

In the Edderachillis district, forming the western portion of what is called Lord Reay's country, a tradition existed to the effect that Wolves were at one time so numerous that to avoid their ravages in disinterring bodies from their graves, the inhabitants were obliged to have recourse to the island of Handa as a safer place of sepulture.‡

The Earl of Ellesmere, referring to an extract from the journal of his son, the Hon. Capt. Francis Egerton, R.N., written in India, and relating to an apparently well authenticated story of some children in Oude who were carried away and brought up by Wolves,§ says : "It is odd that the same tale should extend to the Highlands. I got a story identical in all its particulars of the Wolf time of Sutherland from the old forester of the Reay, in which district Gaelic tradition avers that Wolves so abounded that it was usual to bury the dead in the Island of Handa to avoid desecration of the graves."

* Nimmo's " Stirlingshire," pp. 745, 750.
† Stuart, " Lays of the Deer Forest," ii. p. 221.
‡ Wilson's " Voyage round Scotland," vol. i. p. 346.
§ " Ann. and Mag. Nat. Hist.," second series, viii. p. 153.

There is a tradition on Loch Awe side, Argyllshire, that Green Island was used as a burial-place for the same reason.*

In like manner an island in Loch Maree, Ross-shire, was for the same reason selected for a similar purpose.†

On the western shores of Argyllshire the small isle of St. Mungo, still used as a burial-place, has been appropriated to this purpose from the days when the Wolves were the terror of the land, the passage between it and the mainland opposing a barrier which they in vain attempted to cross.‡

In Athole it was formerly the custom to bury the dead in coffins made of five flagstones to preserve the bodies from Wolves.§

When treating of the Wolf in England it was observed that many names of places compounded of " Wolf " indicate in all probability localities where this animal was at one time common. The same may be said of Scotland. Chalmers cites in Roxburghshire, " Wolf-cleugh " in Roberton parish on Borthwick Water ; "Wolf-cleugh" on Rule Water;" and " Wolf-hope" on Catlee-burn, in Southdean parish ;‖ to which may be added "Wolflee" or "Woole," on Wauchope-burn ; and " Wolfkeilder " on the Northumbrian border. There are also " Wolf-gill land," in the

* This island is still used as a burying-ground. Mr. Harvie Brown saw fresh graves there in May, 1879.
† Macculloch's " Western Isles," quoted in Chambers' " Gazetteer of Scotland," p. 755.
‡ Constable's *Edinburgh Magazine*, Nov. 1817, p. 340.
§ " Statistical Account of Scotland" (1972), vol. ii. p. 465.
‖ Chambers' " Caledonia," vol. ii. p. 132.

parish and shire of Dumfries, and "Wolfstan," in the parish of Pencaitland, East Lothian.*

Craigmaddie, "the rock of the Wolf," in the parish of Baldernock, and Stronachon, "the ridge of the dog," in the parish of Drymen, point by their name to localities in Stirlingshire which were formerly the haunts of the Wolf.

Mr. Hardy states (*l. c.*) that on the farm of Godscroft a cairn, now removed, was called "Wolf-camp." It may have been a Wolf's den, or perhaps an ancient " meet " of the Wolf-hunters who were summoned by the sheriff in the days of the early Kings James.

He adds that in 1769 there was a farm called "Burnbrae" and "Wolfland" in the parish of Nenthorn belonging to Kerr of Fowberry. The name seems to imply that it had been held in former times by the tenure of hunting the Wolf; lands thus granted being called "Wolf-hunt lands," as already remarked under the head of the Wolf in England.

In 1756 Buffon was assured by Lord Morton, then President of the Royal Society, " a Scotsman worthy of the greatest credit and respect, and proprietor of large territories in that country," that Wolves still existed in Scotland at that date.

William Smellie, the translator and editor of Buffon's "Natural History," thus comments on this statement (vol. iv. p. 210, note, 3rd edit., 1791) : "We are fully disposed to give due weight to an authority so respectable and so worthy of credit ; but we are convinced that the Count has misapprehended his

* Hardy, "Proc. Berwickshire Naturalists' Club," 1861, p. 289.

lordship, for it is universally known to the inhabitants of Scotland that not a single Wolf has been seen in any part of that country for more than a century past."

In asserting that this is universally known to the inhabitants of Scotland, the translator and editor has erred in the other extreme, for, as has been already shown, Wolves were killed in Sutherland within fifty years of the date of his remark and within thirteen years of the date mentioned by Buffon.

HISTORICAL EVIDENCE.—IRELAND.

From the scanty and more or less inaccessible nature of the records relating to the natural history of Ireland, compared with what exists in the case of England and Scotland, the result of a search for materials for a history of the Wolf in Ireland has proved less satisfactory than could have been wished. Nevertheless, some curious fragments of information on the subject have been collected from various sources, and are now brought together for the first time.

There is abundant evidence to show that Wolves formerly existed in great numbers in Ireland, and that they maintained their ground for a longer period there than in any other part of the United Kingdom. In bygone ages they must have fared sumptuously amongst the herds of reindeer and Irish elk, which at one time were contemporary with them ; and the discovery of numerous skeletons, often entire herds of deer, imbedded in the mud of ancient lakes, has led to the surmise that these animals probably perished in this way in their attempts to escape from packs of pursuing Wolves.

Giraldus Cambrensis, who lived in the reigns of Henry II., Richard I., and John, and who visited Ireland in 1183 and again in 1185–6, when he accompanied Prince John there, has left a curious account of the wild animals then existing in Ireland, amongst which is included the Wolf. He adds, "the Wolves often have whelps in the month of December, either in consequence of the great mildness of the climate, or rather in token of the evils of treason and rapine, which are rife here before their proper season."*

In the "Polychronicon" of Ranulphus Higden, the monk of Chester, who died about 1360, we have a later account of the Irish fauna, and in this also the Wolf figures. Thus he says :—" *Terra hæc magis vaccis quam bobus, pascuis quam frugibus, gramine quam grano fecunda. Abundat tamen salmonibus, murænis, anguillis, et cæteris marinis piscibus; aquilis quoque, gruibus, pavonibus, coturnicibus, niso, falcone et acciptre generoso. Lupos quoque habet, mures nocentissimos ; sed et araneas, sanguisugas, et lacertas habet innocuas. Mustelas quoque parvi corporis sed valde animosas possidet.*†* This passage is thus rendered by his translator, John Trevisa (A.D. 1357–1387), and adopted by Caxton in his " Cronycles of

<hr>

* "Topographia Hiberniæ," lib. ii. cap. xxvi. p. 726, ed. Dimock, vol. v. p. 112. And not only Wolves, but crows and owls are said to have had young at Christmas. Op. cit., p. 112.

† "Polychronicon Ranulphi Higden, Monachi Cestrensis," ed. Babington (Master of the Rolls Series), vol. i. pp. 334, 335.

England," 1480 :—" In this lond beeth mo kyn than oxen, more pasture than corne, more grass than seed. There is grete plente of samon, of lampreyes, of eles, and of other see fisch : of egles, of cranes, of pekokes, of corlewes, of sparhaukes, of goshaukes, and of gentil faucouns, *and of Wolfes,* and of wel shrewed mys. There beeth attercoppes, blood-soukers, and enettes that dooth noon harm," &c.* Some translators and later copyists have here and there singularly perverted the original meaning of this passage by blunders and mistranslations. Amongst these may be mentioned the author or authors of " The Book of Howth," a small folio in vellum of the sixteenth century, written in different hands, and preserved amongst the Carew MSS. (vol. dcxxiii.), in the Lambeth Library.†

* Some little interest attaches to this passage from the curious assemblage of animals named in it. At the period referred to "cranes" seem to have become common enough in Ireland: "*in tanta vero numerositate se grues ingerunt, ut uno in grege centum, et circiter hunc numerum frequenter invenias*" ("Topog. Hibern.," ed. Dimock, v. 46). By "pekokes" (*pavonibus*), it would seem the capercaillie is intended, "*pavones silvestres hic abundant,*" says Giraldus (tom. cit. p. 47). "*Coturnicibus*" should be rendered "quails," not "curlews." ("*Item coturnicus hic plurimi,*" Girald. v. 47). "*Mures nocentissimos*" are not necessarily shrew-mice, which are insectivorous. In all probability that destructive little animal, the long-tailed field-mouse (*Mus sylvaticus*) is referred to. By reading "araneos" (shrews) for "araneas" (spiders) some confusion is accounted for. " Attercoppes" is the translation of *araneas*. Jamieson, in his " Scottish Dictionary," gives " Atter-cap," " Attircop," spider, with two variants—Northumberland, " Attercop," and Cumberland, "Attercob," a cobweb. A. S. atter coppe, from atter, *venenum*, and copp, *calix*; receiving its denomination partly from its form, and partly from its character; q. a cup of venom. By " bloodsuckers," of course, leeches are meant: for " enettes" *lacertas* we may read "euettes" or " evettes"—*i.e.*, efts, that do no harm.
† *Cf.* Brewer and Bullen, Calendar Carew MSS., "The Book of Howth," p. 31.

Campion, whose "History of Ireland" was published in 1570, refers to the chase of the Wolf there with Wolf-hounds. "The Irish," he says, "are not without Wolves, or greyhounds to hunt them; bigger of bone and limme than a colt."*

Sir James Ware, in his "Antiquities of Ireland" (1658), notices, "those hounds which, from their hunting of Wolves, are commonly called 'Wolf-dogs,'

IRISH WOLF-HOUND.

being creatures of great strength and size, and of a fine shape."

Ray has described the Irish Wolf-hound as a tall, rough greyhound; so also has Pennant, who descants at some length on his extraordinary size and power.

The Wolf-hound here figured is a dog belonging to

* *See* also Holinshed, "Descrip. Irel." 1586; and Camden, "Britannia," vol. ii. p. 1312 (ed. Gibson).

Capt. G. H. Graham, of Rednock, Dursley, Gloucestershire, and bred from the only authentic strain of Irish Wolf-hound now known. His dimensions are as follows :—Height, 29½ in. ; girth, 33½ in. ; length of head, 12 in. ; girth of do. in front of ears, 18¾ in. ; forearm, 8½ in. Weight, 102 lbs.

In a Privy Seal from Henry VIII. to the Lord-Deputy and Council of Ireland,* his Majesty takes notice of the suit of the Duke of Albuquerque, of Spain (of the Privy Council to Henry VIII.), on behalf of the Marquis Desarrya and his son, " that it might please his Majesty to grant to the said Marquis and his son, and the longer liver of them, yearly, out of Ireland, two goshawks, and four Wolf-hounds," and commands the Deputy for the time being to order the delivery of the hawks and hounds, and to charge the cost to the Treasury.

In November, 1562, as we learn from the State Papers relating to Ireland,† the Irish chieftain, Shane O'Neill, forwarded to Queen Elizabeth, through Robert Dudley, Earl of Leicester, a present of two horses, two hawks, and two Irish Wolf-dogs. In 1585, Sir John Perrott, who was Lord-Deputy of Ireland from January, 1584, to July, 1588,‡ sent to Sir Francis Walsingham, then Secretary of State in London, " a brace of good Wolf-dogs, one black, the other white."

Again, in 1608, we find that Irish Wolf-hounds were sent from Ireland by Captain Esmond, of

* Rot. Canc. Dec. 9, 36 H. 8, *dorso.*
† Eliz., vol. vii. No. 40, in Pub. Rec. Off.   ‡ Eliz., vol. cxx. No. 12.

Duncannon, to Gilbert, seventh Earl of Shrews-bury.*

These dogs were considered very valuable, and were highly thought of by those who received them as presents; but some years later, when, owing to the great increase in the number of Wolves in some parts of Ireland, their services were more than ever required to keep down these ferocious animals, a law, presently to be noticed, was passed to prohibit their exportation.

About this time George Turbervile, a gentleman of Dorsetshire, was writing his " Booke of Hunting,"† in which, referring to this animal, he says :—" The Wolf is a beaste sufficiently known in France and other countries where he is bred ; but here in England they be not to be found in any place. In Ireland, as I have heard, there are great store of them ; and because many noblemen and gentlemen have a desire to bring that countrie to be inhabited and civilly governed (and would God there were more of the same mind), therefore I have thought good to set down the nature and manner of hunting the Wolf according to mine author."‡ He then proceeds to describe the mode then in vogue of hunting this animal. An open spot was generally chosen, at some distance from the great coverts where the Wolves were known to lie, and here, in concealment, a brace, sometimes two brace, of Wolf-hounds were

* " Archæol. Æliana," vol. ii. p. 226.

† " Imprinted at London for Christopher Barker at the signe of the Grashopper in Paules Churchyarde.   Anno 1575."

‡ Jacques de Fouilloux, " Traité de Vénerie."

placed. A horse was killed, and the fore-quarters were trailed through the paths and ways in the wood during the previous day, and back to where the carcase lay, and there they were left. When night approached, out came the Wolves, and having struck the scent, they followed it until they found the dead horse, when of course they began to feed on the flesh, and early in the morning, just before daybreak, the hunters placed their dogs so as to prevent the Wolves from returning to cover. When a Wolf came to the spot, the men in charge of the Wolf-hounds suffered him to pass by the first, but the last were let slip full in his face, and at the same instant the others were let slip also, so that, the first staying him ever so little, he was sure to be attacked on all sides at once, and therefore, the more easily taken.*

In Robert Legge's "Book of Information," compiled in 1584 by order of Sir John Perrott, the above-named Lord-Deputy of Ireland, "for the information of the civil government of that realm," it is recommended, *inter alia*, that for the "destruction of ravening and devouring Wolves, some order might be had, as when any lease is granted, to put in some clause that the tenant endeavour himself to spoil and kill Wolves with traps, snares, or such devices as he may devise."†

* The most complete account which we have met with of Wolf-hunting in modern times is that given by Col. Thornton in his "Sporting Tour through various parts of France in 1802," vol. i. pp. xxi–xxxix. A more recent treatise, however, has been published under the title of "Wolf-hunting in Brittany."

† Carew MSS., vol. dcvii. p. 115. Brewer and Bullen, Calendar of Carew MSS., Eliz., p. 401.

About this time, it is said, Wolves committed great devastation amongst the flocks in Munster. After the destruction of Kilmallock by James Fitzmaurice, in 1591, that place is stated to have become the haunt of Wolves.

For some account of their ravages during Desmond's rebellion, the reader may be referred to O'Sullivan's "Compendium Historiæ Catholicæ Hiberniæ," 1621 (lib. viii. cap. 6).

At a later period, according to Fynes Moryson, who was Secretary to Lord-Deputy Mountjoy, and who wrote a "History of Ireland from 1599 to 1603," the cattle had to be driven in at night, "for fear of thieves (the Irish using almost no other kind of theft), or else for fear of Wolves, the destruction whereof being neglected by the inhabitants, oppressed with greater mischiefs, they are so much grown in numbers as sometimes on winter nights they will come and prey in villages and the suburbs of cities."*

In May, 1594, Lord William Russell was appointed Lord-Deputy of Ireland by Queen Elizabeth. From entries in his "Journal," extending from "June 24, 1594, to May 27, 1597,"† it appears that both he and Lady Russell, who accompanied him to Ireland, frequently participated in the pleasures of the chase, and amused themselves at different times with hawking, fishing, and hunting. Under date May 26, 1596, it is recorded : " My Lord and Lady rode

* Moryson, "Hist. Ireland," Dublin ed., 1735, vol. ii. p. 367.
† Preserved amongst the Carew MSS. at Lambeth Palace, vol. dcxii.

abroad a hunting the Wolf." As the Vice-regal Court was then located at Kilmainham, almost within the city of Dublin, it would appear that the Wolf in question was to be found at no great distance beyond the city walls,

Sir Arthur Chichester, writing to Sir John Davys, March 31, 1609, in reference to the pending plantation of Ulster, incidentally remarks, that "if the Irish do not possess and inhabit a great part of the lands in some of those escheated countries, none but Wolves and wild beasts would possess them for many years to come; for where civil men may have lands for reasonable rents in so many thousand places in that province, and in this whole kingdom, they will not plant themselves in mountains, rocks and desert places, though they might have the land for nothing."*

In the reign of James I. it would seem that active measures were advised for the destruction of Wolves in Ireland, and the following "Heads of a Bill in the Irish Parliament, 1611," will be found preserved amongst the Carew MSS., formerly in the Record Office, but now at Lambeth Palace :† "An Act for killing Wolves and other vermin, touching the days of hunting, the people that are to attend, who to be their director, an inhibition not to use any arms. The Lord Deputy or Principal Governor to prohibit such hunting if he suspect that such assemblies by colour of hunting may prove inconvenient."

* State Papers, Ireland, in Record Office, vol. ccxxvi, 58.
† Carew, MSS., vol. dcxxix. p. 35. *See* also Hamilton's " Calendar of State Papers referring to Ireland," Jac. I., sub anno, p. 192.

This proposed Act, however, seems never to have become law, for no mention of it is made in the eight volumes of Irish Statutes published by authority in Dublin in 1765. It is not surprising therefore that the ravages of the Wolves in Ireland continued. In 1619 their numbers in Ulster compelled people "to house their cattle in the bawnes of their castles, where all the winter nights they stood up to their bellies in dirt. Another reason is to prevent thieves and false-hearted brethren who have spies abroad, and will come thirty miles out of one province into another to practise a cunning robbery."*

Howell, in one of his "Familiar Letters," written to Sir James Crofts, September 6th, 1624, says :—A pleasant tale I heard Sir Thomas Fairfax relate of a souldier in Ireland, who having got his passport to go for England, as he past through a wood with his knapsack upon his back, being weary, he sate down under a tree wher he open'd his knapsack and fell to some victuals he had ; but upon a sudden he was surpriz'd with two or three *Woolfs*, who, coming towards him, he threw them scraps of bread and cheese till all was done; then the *Woolfs* making a nearer approach unto him, he knew not what shift to make, but by taking a pair of bagpipes which he had, and as soon as he began to play upon them, the *Woolfs* ran all away as if they had been scar'd out of their wits. Whereupon the souldier said, "A pox take you all, if I had known you had lov'd musick so well, you should have had it before dinner !"

* Gainsford's "Glory of England," p. 148.

In 1641 and 1652 Wolves were particularly trouble-some in Ireland, and in the latter year the following Order in Council was issued by Cromwell, prohibiting the exportation of Wolf-dogs :—

" *Declaration against transporting of Wolfe Dogges.*

" Forasmuch as we are credibly informed that Wolves doe much increase and destroy many cattle in several partes of this Dominion, and that some of the enemie's party, who have laid down armes, and have liberty to go beyond sea and others, do attempt to carry away such great dogges as are commonly called *Wolfe dogges;* whereby the breed of them which are useful for destroying of Wolves would (if not prevented) speedily decay. These are therefore to prohibit all persons whatsoever from exporting any of the said dogges out of this Dominion; and searchers and other officers of the Customs, in the several partes and creekes of this Dominion, are hereby strictly required to seize and make stopp of all such dogges, and deliver them either to the com-mon huntsman, appointed for the precinct where they are seized upon, or to the governor of the said precinct.

"*Dated at* KILKENNY, *April* 27, 1652."

The following year another Order in Council was made which ran as follows :—

" *Declaration touching Wolves.*

" For the better destroying of Wolves, which of late years have much increased in most parts of this nation, it is ordered that the Commanders in Chiefe and Commissioners of the Revenue in the several precincts doe consider of, use, and execute all good wayes and meanes how the Wolves in the counties and places within the respective precincts may be taken and destroyed; and to employ such person or persons, and to appoint such daies and tymes for hunting the Wolfe, as they shall adjudge necessary. And it is further ordered that all such person or persons as shall take, kill, or destroy any Wolfes and shall bring forth the head of the Wolfe before the said commanders of the revenue, shall receive the sums following, viz., for every bitch Wolfe, six pounds;* for every dog Wolfe, five pounds; for every cubb which preyeth for himself, forty shillings; for every suckling cubb, ten shillings. And no Wolfe after the last September until the 10th January be accounted a young Wolfe, and the Commissioners of the Revenue shall cause the same to be equallie assessed within their precincts.

" DUBLIN, *June* 29, 1653."†

The assessments here ordered fell heavily in some districts. Thus in December, 1665, the inhabitants of Mayo county petitioned the Council of State that the Commissioners of Assessment might be at liberty

* The price paid in Sutherlandshire, in 1621, was 6*l.* 13*s.* 4*d.* See p. 169.

† These documents were extracted from the original Privy Council Book of Cromwell's government in Ireland, preserved in Dublin Castle and are quoted by Hardiman in his edition of O'Flaherty's " West or H'Iar Connaught," p. 180.

to compound for Wolf-heads; which was ordered accordingly.

In 1662, as appears by the Journal of the House of Commons, Sir John Ponsonby reported from the Committee of Grievances that a Bill should be brought in "to encourage the killing of Wolves and foxes in Ireland."

In the "Travels of the Grand Duke Cosmo III. in England," 1669 (p. 103), the author speaks of Wolves as common in Ireland, "for the hunting of which the dogs called 'mastiffs' are in great request."

O'Flaherty, in his "West or H'Iar Connaught" (1684), enumerates the wild animals which were to be found in that district in his day, and names " *Wolves*, deere, foxes, badgers, hedgehogs, hares, rabbets, squirrells, martens, weesles, and the amphibious otter, of which kind the white-faced otter is very rare." Hardiman, in a note to his edition of this work (1846), says: "When our author wrote (1684), and for some years afterwards, wolves were to be found in Iar Connaught, but not in such numbers as in the early part of that century. The last Wolf which I have been able to trace here was killed in the mountains of Joyce country, in the year 1700. After the wars of 1641 the ravages of the Wolves were so great throughout Ireland as to excite the attention of the State. 'Wolf-hunters' were appointed in various districts, and amongst others in Iar Connaught, who helped to rid the country of these ferocious animals."*

* Hardiman, op. cit., p. 10, note.

In an account of the British Islands, published at Nuremberg in 1690, the wilds of Kerry are referred to as harbouring Wolves and foxes;* and in the reign of William and Mary, Ireland was sometimes called by the nickname of "Wolf-land." Thus in a poem on the Battle of La Hogue, 1692, called "Advice to a Painter," the terror of the Irish army is described :—

A chilling damp,
And Wolf-land howl runs through the rising camp.

"Three places in Ireland are commemorated, each as having had the last Irish wolf killed there—namely, one in the south, another near Glenarm, and the third, Wolf-hill, three miles from Belfast."† The one in the south is probably that referred to in Edwards's "Cork Remembrancer" (p. 131), wherein the following entry occurs : "This year (1710) the last presentment [to the Grand Jury] for killing wolves was made in the county of Cork."‡ In the old "Statistical Account of Scotland," however, edited by Sir John Sinclair, it is stated (vol. xii. p. 447) that the last was killed in Ireland in 1709.

The great woods of Shillela, on the confines of Carlow and Wicklow, now the property of Earl Fitzwilliam, are said to have held Wolves until about the year 1700, when the last of them was destroyed in the neighbourhood of Glendaloch.§

* This work we have not seen. It is quoted by Macaulay, in his "History of England," vol. iii. p. 136.
† Thompson, "Nat. Hist., Ireland," vol. iv. p. 34.
‡ See also Scouler, "Journ. Geol. Soc.," Dublin, vol. i. p. 226.
§ Mackenzie's "Natural History," p 20. This volume, published in London in modern times, is undated.

In a poem, in six cantos, published as late as 1719, and entitled, "MacDermot, or the Irish Fortune-Hunter," "Wolf-hunting" and "Wolf-spearing" are represented as common sports in Munster. Here is an extract :—

It happen'd on a day with horn and hounds,
A baron gallop'd through MacDermot's grounds,
Well hors'd, pursuing o'er the dusty plain
A Wolf that sought the neighbouring woods to gain:
Mac hears th' alarm, and, with his oaken spear,
Joins in the chase, and runs before the peer,
Outstrips the huntsman, dogs, and panting steeds,
And, struck by him, the falling savage bleeds.

The crest of the O'Quins of Munster is "a Wolf's head, erased, argent," possibly perpetuating the prowess of some former noted Wolf-hunter in that ancient family.

The author of "The Present State of Great Britain and Ireland," printed in London in 1738, wrote at that date, "Wolves still abound too much in Ireland; they pray for the Wolves, least they should devour them."

In Smith's "Ancient and Modern State of the County of Kerry," 1756 (of which book Macaulay said, "I do not know that I have ever met with a better book of the kind and of the size," "Hist. Eng." iii. 136), the author, speaking of certain ancient enclosures, observes (p. 173) that many of them were made to secure cattle from *Wolves*, which animals were not entirely extirpated until about the year 1710, as I find by presentments for raising money for destroying them in some old grand-jury books."

Traces of old circular entrenchments, into which

cattle and sheep were driven for protection from Wolves, are still to be seen in many parts of Ireland, especially in the south. One of these, in the county Tyrone, will be noticed presently.

In Harris's edition of Sir James Ware's "Works" (Dublin, 1764), the editor, commenting upon the passage, "1 shall but just hint at the eagerness of the Irish in the chase, as in hunting Wolves and stags," remarks in a footnote (p. 165), "So said in the year 1658. But there are no Wolves in Ireland now." This statement in turn may be controverted upon very respectable authority, but the conflict of evidence renders it very difficult to fix with certainty the precise date at which the animal became extinct.

The following account is given of the destruction, by a noted Wolf-hunter, of the last Wolves in the county Tyrone :—

" In the mountainous parts of the county Tyrone, the inhabitants suffered much from Wolves, and gave as much for the head of one of these animals as they would now give (1829) for the capture of a notorious robber on the highway. There lived in those days an adventurer who, alone and unassisted, made it his occupation to destroy those ravagers. The time for attacking them was at night. There was a species of dog kept for the purpose of hunting them, resembling a rough, stout, half-bred greyhound, but much stronger.

" In the county Tyrone there was then a large space of ground enclosed by a high stone wall, having a gap at the two opposite extremities, and in this were secured the flocks of the surrounding farmers. Still, secure though this fold was deemed, it was entered by the Wolves, and its inmates slaughtered.

" The neighbouring proprietors having heard of the noted Wolf-hunter above mentioned, by name Rory Carragh, sent for him and offered the usual reward, with some addition, if he would undertake to destroy the two remaining Wolves that had committed such devastation. Carragh, undertaking the task, took with him two Wolf dogs and a little boy, the only person he could prevail on to accompany him, and, at the approach of night, repaired to the fold in question.

" ' Now,' said Carragh to the boy, ' as the Wolves usually attack the opposite extremities of the sheep-fold at the same time, I must leave you and one of the dogs to guard this one, while I go to the other. He steals with all the caution of a cat; nor will you hear him, but the dog will, and will positively give him the first fall. If you are not active when he is down, to rivet his neck to the ground with this spear, he will rise up and kill both you and the dog.'

" ' I'll do what I can,' said the boy, as he took the spear from the Wolf-hunter's hand.

" The boy immediately threw open the gate of the fold, and took his seat in the inner part, close to the entrance, his faithful companion crouching at his side and seeming perfectly aware of the dangerous business he was engaged in. The night was very dark and cold, and the poor little boy being benumbed with the chilly air, was beginning to fall into a kind of sleep, when at that instant the dog, with a roar, leaped across him and laid his mortal enemy upon the earth. The boy was roused into double activity by the voice of his companion, and drove the spear through the Wolf's neck, as he had been directed ; at which time Carragh made his appearance with the head of the other."*

In an interesting article on the Irish Wolf-dog, published in *The Irish Penny Journal* for 1841 (p. 354), the writer says :†—"I am at present acquainted with an old gentleman between eighty and ninety years of age, whose mother remembered Wolves to have been killed in the county of Wexford about the years 1730–40, and it is asserted by many persons of weight and veracity that a Wolf was killed in the Wicklow mountains so recently as 1770.

A few years since, Sir J. Emerson Tennent wrote on this subject as follows :—

"Waringstown, in the county of Down, on the confines of the county of Armagh, takes its name from the family of Waring, which, in the reign of Queen Mary, fled to Ireland from Lancashire to avoid the persecution of the Lollards. At the close of the seventeenth century the Waring of that day was a member of the Irish Parliament ; and his eldest son, Samuel Waring, was born about the year 1699, and

---

* "The Biography of a Tyrone Family " (Belfast, 1829), p. 74.
† This article, published under the initials of H. D. R., has since been admitted to have been written by H. D. Richardson, author of " The Dog : its Origin, Natural History, and Varieties," in which work it has been embodied with additions, 1848.

died at a very advanced age in 1793. He was succeeded by his nephew, the Very Reverend Holt Waring, Dean of Dromore, who was born in 1766, and whom I had the honour to know. With him I happened to be travelling through the Mourne mountains, in the county of Down, on our way to the Earl of Roden's, about the year 1834 or 1835, when the conversation turning upon the social condition of Ireland in the previous century, he told me that a foal belonging to his uncle had been killed by a Wolf in the stable at Waringstown, and that he, when a boy, had heard the occurrence repeatedly adverted to in the family circle. The dean was a man of singularly acute mind and accurate memory, and unless this statement of his be altogether a delusion, this would seem to be the last recorded appearance of a Wolf in Ireland."

The last piece of evidence collected has reference to a communication which appeared in *The Zoologist* for 1862 (p. 7996), under the heading, "Wolf Days of Ireland." On applying to the writer, Mr. Jonathan Grubb, of Sudbury, for further particulars, he obligingly replied in a letter, dated June 6, 1877, as follows :—

"I am now in my seventieth year. My father, who was born in 1767, used to tell the Wolf stories to us when we were children. His mother—my grandmother—related them to him. She was born in 1731. Her maiden name was Malone ; and her uncles, from whom she received her information, were the actors in the scenes described at Ballyroggin, county Kildare. She remembered one of them,

James Malone, telling her how his brother came home one night on horseback pursued by a pack of Wolves, who overtook him, and continued leaping on to the hind quarters of his horse till he reached his own door, crying out, ' Oh ! James, James ! my horse is ate with the Wolves.' "

The precise date of this occurrence cannot now be fixed ; but it seems plain that Wolves existed in Kildare during the first quarter of the eighteenth century, and perhaps as late as 1721.

To sum up. So far as can be now ascertained, it appears that the Wolf became extinct in England during the reign of Henry VII. ; that it survived in Scotland until 1743; and that the last of these animals was killed in Ireland, according to Richardson, in 1770, or, according to Sir James Emerson Tennent, subsequently to 1766.

In the foregoing observations, no reference has been made to " Were-wolves," nor has any matter been introduced touching the fabulous or superstitious aspect of the Wolf's history in the British Islands. All such allusions have been purposely avoided, in order to confine the subject within reasonable limits.

Before concluding, however, we may perhaps be excused for citing so respectable an authority as Sir Thomas Browne, who, in his " Enquiries into Vulgar and Common Errors," has alluded to the popular notion that Wolves cannot live in England.

In vol. iii. p. 344, of his " Works " (Wilkin's edition), he says :—" Thus because there are no Wolves in England, nor have been observed for divers generations (1646), common people have proceeded into opinions, and some wise men into affirmations, that they will not live therein, although brought from other countries."

He also notices the popular belief that "a Wolf first seeing a man begets a dumbness in him," a notion as old as the time of Pliny, who wrote: " *In Italia, ut creditur, luporum visus est noxius, vocemque homini, quem prius contemplatur adimere.*" In France, when anyone becomes hoarse, the say " *Il a vu le loup.*"*

" The ground or occasional original thereof," says Sir Thomas Browne,† " was probably the amazement and sudden silence the unexpected appearance of Wolves doth often put upon travellers, not by a supposed vapour or venomous emanation, but a vehement fear, which naturally produceth obmutescence, and sometimes irrecoverable silence."

A critic, adverting to this passage, has somewhat wittily remarked : " Dr. Browne did unadvisedly reckon this among his vulgar errors, for I believe he would find this no error if he were suddenly surprised by a wolf, having no means to escape or save himself ! "

* Howell's " Familiar Letters," vol. ii. p. 52.
† Op. cit., vol. ii. p. 422.